Crochet
On the Double™
Made Easy

Table of
Contents

Table of Contents

Editor DONNA SCOTT
Acquisitions Editor DEBORAH LEVY-HAMBURG
Technical Editor SHARON LOTHROP
Copy Editor SHIRLEY PATRICK
Book Design GREG SMITH
Production Artist JOANNE GONZALEZ
Production Supervisor MINETTE SMITH
Photography Supervisor SCOTT CAMPBELL
Photographer ANDY J. BURNFIELD
Photo Department Assistants MARTHA COQUAT
CRYSTAL KEY

Chief Executive Officer JOHN ROBINSON
Publishing Director DAVID J. McKEE
Book Marketing Manager CRAIG SCOTT
Editorial Director VIVIAN ROTHE
Product Development Manager CONNIE ELLISON
Publishing Services Manager ANGE VAN ARMAN

Customer Service 1-800-449-0440
Pattern Services (903) 636-5140

ISBN: 1-57367-126-6
First Printing: 2003
Library of Congress Catalog Card Number:
2002109897

Printed in the United States of America.

Visit us at
NeedlecraftShop.com
or
CrochetBooksOnline.com

Every effort has been made to ensure the accuracy
and completeness of the instructions in this book.
However, we cannot be responsible for human error or for
the results when using materials other than those specified
in the instructions, or for variations in individual work.

Welcome!

Like many of you, we had always heard of the old "cro-hooking" technique that used a double-ended crochet hook to create a different type of fabric unlike conventional types of crochet. With a look similar to knitting, this softly-textured fabric had the added bonus of being reversible as well.

This double-ended hook technique has been around for a long time, with some of the first published patterns featuring this method of crochet having appeared in the early 1900s. It has continued to maintain its place among other crochet trends that have developed over the years, but it has never been as exciting or versatile as it is today.

Thanks to the creative genius of leading crochet designers, the old-fashioned technique of "cro-hooking" has been transformed into one of today's most intriguing and inspiring forms of crochet.

The double-ended crochet method is now growing by leaps and bounds in popularity and taking the art of crochet to new heights in style and versatility. It's a prime example of the old adage "what's old is new," and it's better than ever!

Even if you've never experienced the enjoyment of working patterns with a double-ended crochet hook, the fabulous projects we've chosen for this book, all stitched using the Crochet on the Double™ and Crochenit™ techniques, will entice you to jump right in and get started.

Within these pages, you'll find smartly styled wraps for all occasions, wonderful wearables with fashionable flair, cuddly sweet treasures for babies and children, holiday delights to make Christmas sparkle and creative home accents to decorate in style.

You'll be amazed at how easy it is and the beautiful, finished results you can achieve even with only a few basic stitches. Once begun, the fast-and-fun double-ended technique is hard to resist!

Enjoy!

The Editors

Crochet on the Double™

The basic Crochet On the Double stitch pattern is usually worked with two colors, with the colors used alternately for every other row. Using two skeins of the same color will create a solid pattern, and other combinations can be made using a variety of colors.

There are two basic stitches used in Crochet On the Double: working through the vertical bars and working through the horizontal bars. Working through the vertical bars, which is similar to the afghan stitch, produces a think, spongy fabric like a knitted garter stitch. Working through the horizontal bars elongates the stitches and spreads the rows apart, giving the fabric a softer feel, yet keeping the ridged garter stitch effect.

The step-by-step photos below will help you master these two basic stitch patterns.

The Crochet On the Double hooks and Crochet On the Double swivel hooks are available in sizes G, H and K and can be purchased from local craft, fabric and variety stores or from the Annie's Attic Needlecraft Catalog by calling 1-800-582-6643 or by visiting AnniesAttic.com.

Insert hook in second chain from hook, yarn over and draw through (see photo A), leaving loop on hook.

Holding the double-end hook like a knife makes it easier to use.

A

*To **draw up a loop,** insert hook in next chain, yarn over and draw through; repeat from * across (see photo B), leaving all loops on hook.

B

Drop color A, turn hook and slide all loops to opposite end of hook (see photo C).

*Each of these loops counts as a stitch and is referred to as a **vertical bar**.*

C

To **work loops off hook,** with color B, place slip knot on hook (see photo D);

D

draw slip knot through first loop on hook (see photo E).

E

Pulling the slip knot through the first loop makes the first stitch of the row.

Yarn over, draw through next 2 loops on hook (see photo F);

*When you pull through the 2 loops in this step, you will go through one loop of each color. The stitches you are making in this step are referred to as **Horizontal Bar**.*

F

to **work remaining loops off hook,** (yarn over, draw through next 2 loops on hook) across, leaving last loop on hook (see photo G), **do not turn.**

You will now have only one loop on your hook. This loop counts as the first vertical bar of the next row. Never turn after working the loops off your hook.

Skip first vertical bar, insert hook under next vertical bar, yarn over and draw up a loop (see photo H);

draw up a loop in each vertical bar across, drop color B (see photo I);

If you have trouble with your loops falling off the hook, cap the unused end with a rubber knit stopper or a piece of cork.

turn and slide all loops to opposite end of hook (see photo J).

To keep your yarn from tangling when you turn, rotate your hook back and forth rather than in a circle.

Pick up color A from row below, yarn over and draw through first loop on hook (see photo K);

This is the same process as in step E, except you are using the yarn from the row below rather than placing a slip knot on the hook.

yarn over, draw through next 2 loops on hook (see photo L).

Remember to go through one loop of each color when working the loops off in this step.

To **work remaining loops off hook,** (yarn over and draw through next 2 loops on hook) across, leaving last loop on hook, **do not turn** (see photo M).

Skip first vertical bar, draw up loop in next vertical bar (see photo N), draw up loop in each bar across, drop color A, turn. Slide all loops to opposite end of hook.

Continue alternating colors until ending with color A (or color specified in individual pattern instructions).

Skip first vertical bar, slip stitch (or use the stitch called for in the individual pattern instructions) across (see photo O). Fasten off.♦

*T*he Crochenit hook is used with stitch patterns designed specially for the double-ended hook technique, and its fun-to-use size makes projects work up quickly. The resulting Crochenit fabric has a look and feel that is much softer than crochet, with a resilient softness that resembles knitting. There's no gauge to worry about, and it's exciting to mix and match all weights of yarns from extra-thick wool to delicate thread. Several weights of yarn can even be used in the same project!

Use the red and green stoppers to help you keep track of when you turn your hook and which end of the hook you work with on any row. As you turn your hook each time, remove the stopper and place it on the opposite end of the hook. Before you lay your work aside, work until you have loops on the hook. Turn the hook, place the green stopper on the end of the hook with which you will begin next time, and place the red stopper on the other end. Red means "Stop" and green means "Go!"

Each Crochenit sequence includes two rows: Row 1 picks up the loops, and Row 2 works them off with the new color. The step-by-step photos and instructions below will help get you started learning the fast-and-easy Crochenit technique.

The Crochenit hook and the Crochenit Cable Hook can be purchased from local craft, fabric and variety stores or from the Annie's Attic Needlecraft Catalog by calling 1-800-582-6643 or by visiting AnniesAttic.com

With color A, insert hook in second chain from hook, yarn over, draw loop through *(see photo A)* leaving loop on hook.

To **draw up a loop,** insert hook in next chain, yarn over, draw loop through; continue in same manner across foundation chain leaving all loops on hook *(see photo B).*

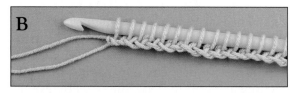

Drop color A, but do not cut yarn. Turn hook; remove stopper and place on opposite end of hook. Slide all loops down to open end of hook *(see photo C).*

NOTE: *When working the Basic Stitch, at this point you will have the same number of loops as your original chain. Each of these loops counts as a stitch, and in the next row each loop will be referred to as a vertical bar.*

To **work loops off hook**, make a slip knot with color B, place slip knot on hook *(see photo D);*

draw slip knot through first loop on hook *(see photo E).*

NOTE: *Pulling the slip knot through the first loop makes the first stitch of the row.*

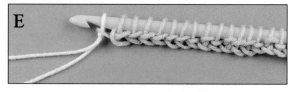

Yarn over, draw through next 2 loops on hook *(see photo F);*

NOTE: *When you draw through the next 2*

loops on hook in this step, you will draw through one loop of each color.

yarn over, draw through next 2 loops on hook; continue in this manner across, leaving last loop on hook *(see photo G);* **do not turn** hook at end of this row.

NOTE: Here's a good rule of thumb to help you remember when to turn the hook. If you have loops on the hook, it's time to turn and change colors. If you have only one loop on the hook at the end of a row, **do not turn;** *work next row with the same color you're working with.*

Skip first vertical bar, insert hook under next vertical bar, yarn over and draw up a loop *(see photo H);*

draw up a loop in each vertical bar across *(see photo I).*

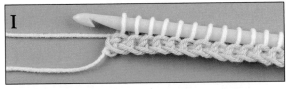

Drop color B but do not cut. Turn hook; remove stopper and place on opposite end of hook. Slide all loops down to open end of hook *(see photo J).*

NOTES: You should now have one strand of yarn hanging from each side of work on hook.

You have now worked a complete sequence of basic stitch. Each Crochenit™ sequence includes two rows: Row 1 picks up the loops, and Row 2 works them off with the new color.

Pick up color A, yarn over and draw through first loop on hook *(see photo K);*

NOTE: This is the same process as the beginning of row 2, except you are using yarn left hanging on row below rather than beginning with a slip knot. As you work the first loop, pull slack out for a nice even edge to your work.

yarn over, (draw through next 2 loops on hook) across, **do not turn.**

NOTE: Remember to draw through one loop of each color each time. At end of row, you will have one loop on hook (see photo L).

Skip first vertical bar, draw up loop in next vertical bar *(see photo M);*

draw up loop in each vertical bar across, drop blue, turn hook; remove stopper and place on opposite end of hook. Slide all loops down to open end of hook.

Continue alternating colors until ending with color A (or color specified in individual pattern instructions).

Skip first vertical bar, slip stitch (or use the stitch called for in the individual pattern instructions) across. Fasten off.♦

Chain (ch)
Yo, draw hook through lp.

Slip Stitch (sl st)
Insert hook in st, yo, draw through st and lp on hook.

Single Crochet (sc)
Insert hook in st, yo, draw lp through, yo, draw through both lps on hook.

Standard Stitch Abbreviations

ch(s)	chain(s)
dc	double crochet
dtr	double treble crochet
hdc	half double crochet
lp(s)	loop(s)
rnd(s)	round(s)
sc	single crochet
sl st	slip stitch
sp(s)	space(s)
st(s)	stitch(es)
tog	together
tr	treble crochet
tr tr/ttr	triple treble crochet
yo	yarn over

Half Double Crochet (hdc)
Yo, insert hook in st, yo, draw lp through, yo, draw through all 3 lps on hook.

Double Crochet (dc)
Yo, insert hook in st, yo, draw lp through, (yo, draw through 2 lps on hook) 2 times.

Treble Crochet (tr)
Yo 2 times, insert hook in st, yo, draw lp through, (yo, draw through 2 lps on hook) 3 times.

Front Loop/ Back Loop
(front lp/back lp)

Single Crochet Color Change (sc color change)
Drop first color; yo with 2nd color, draw through last 2 lps of st.

Reverse Single Crochet (reverse sc)
Working from left to right, insert hook in next st to the right (a), yo, draw through st, complete as sc (b).

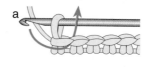

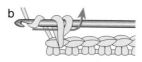

Front Post/Back Post Stitches (fp/bp)
Yo, insert hook from front to back or back to front around post of st on indicated row; complete as stated in pattern.

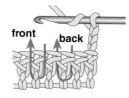

Single Crochet next 2 stitches together (sc next 2 sts tog)
Draw up lp in each of next 2 sts, yo, draw through all 3 lps on hook.

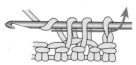

Half Double Crochet next 2 stitches together (hdc next 2 sts tog)
(Yo, insert hook in next st, yo, draw lp through) 2 times, yo, draw through all 5 lps on hook.

Double Crochet next 2 stitches together (dc next 2 sts tog)
(Yo, insert hook in next st, yo, draw lp through, yo, draw through 2 lps on hook) 2 times, yo, draw through all 3 lps on hook.

The patterns in this book are written using American crochet stitch terminology. For our international customers, hook sizes, stitches and yarn definitions should be converted as follows:		But, as with all patterns, test your gauge (tension) to be sure.

US	= UK	Thread/Yarns	Crochet Hooks			
			Metric	US	Metric	US
sl st (slip stitch)	= sc (single crochet)	Bedspread Weight = No. 10 Cotton or Virtuoso	.60mm	14	3.00mm	D/3
sc (single crochet)	= dc (double crochet)	Sport Weight = 4 Ply or thin DK	.75mm	12	3.50mm	E/4
hdc (half double crochet)	= htr (half treble crochet)	Worsted Weight = Thick DK or Aran	1.00mm	10	4.00mm	F/5
dc (double crochet)	= tr (treble crochet)	Measurements	1.50mm	6	4.50mm	G/6
tr (treble crochet)	= dtr (double treble crochet)	1" = 2.54 cm	1.75mm	5	5.00mm	H/8
dtr (double treble crochet)	= ttr (triple treble crochet)	1 yd. = .9144 m	2.00mm	B/1	5.50mm	I/9
skip	= miss	1 oz. = 28.35 g	2.50mm	C/2	6.00mm	J/10

Yarn and Hooks

Always use the weight of yarn specified in the pattern so you can be assured of achieving the proper gauge. It is best to purchase extra of each color needed to allow for differences in tension and dyes.

The hook size stated in the pattern is to be used as a guide. Always work a swatch of the stitch pattern with the suggested hook size. If you find your gauge is smaller or larger than what is specified, choose a different size hook.

Gauge

Gauge is measured by counting the number of rows or stitches per inch. Each of the patterns featured in this book will have a gauge listed. Gauge for some small motifs or flowers is given as an overall measurement. Proper gauge must be attained for the project to come out the size stated and to prevent ruffling and puckering.

Make a swatch in the stitch indicated in the gauge section of the instructions. Lay the swatch flat and measure the stitches. If you have more stitches per inch than specified in the pattern, your gauge is too tight and you need a larger hook. Fewer stitches per inch indicates a gauge that is too loose. In this case, choose a smaller hook size. Next, check the number of rows. If necessary, adjust your row gauge slightly by pulling the loops down a little tighter on your hook, or by pulling the loops up slightly to extend them.

Once you've attained the proper gauge, you're ready to start your project. Remember to check your gauge periodically to avoid problems later.

Pattern Repeat Symbols

Written crochet instructions typically include symbols such as parentheses, asterisks and brackets. In some patterns a diamond or bullet (dot) may be added.

( ) Parentheses enclose instructions which are to be worked again later or the number of times indicated after the parentheses. For example, "(2 dc in next st, skip next st) 5 times" means to follow the instructions within the parentheses a total of five times. If no number appears after the parentheses, you will be instructed when to repeat further into the pattern. Parentheses may also be used to enclose a group of stitches which should be worked in one space or stitch. For example, "(2 dc, ch 2, 2 dc) in next st" means to work all the stitches within the parentheses in the next stitch.

* Asterisks may be used alone or in pairs, usually in combination with parentheses. If used in pairs, the instructions enclosed within asterisks will be followed by instructions for repeating. These repeat instructions may appear later in the pattern or immediately after the last asterisk. For example, "*Dc in next 4 sts, (2 dc, ch 2, 2 dc) in corner sp*, dc in next 4 sts; repeat between ** 2 more times" means to work through the instructions up to the word "repeat," then repeat only the instructions that are enclosed within the asterisks twice.

If used alone, an asterisk marks the beginning of instructions which are to be repeated. Work through the instructions from the beginning, then repeat only the portion after the * up to the word "repeat"; then follow any remaining instructions. If a number of times is given, work through the instructions one time, repeat the number of times stated, then follow the remainder of the instructions.

[ ] Brackets, ◊ diamonds and • bullets are used in the same manner as asterisks. Follow the specific instructions given when repeating.

Finishing

Patterns that require assembly will suggest a tapestry needle in the materials. This should be a #16, #18 or #26 blunt-tipped tapestry needle. When stitching pieces together, be careful to keep the seams flat so pieces do not pucker.

Hiding loose ends is never a fun task, but if done correctly, may mean the difference between an item looking great for years or one that quickly shows signs of wear. Always leave 6-8" of yarn when beginning or ending. Thread the loose end into your tapestry needle and carefully weave through the back of several stitches. Then, weave in the opposite direction, going through different strands. Gently pull the end and clip, allowing the end to pull up under the stitches.

If your project needs blocking, a light steam pressing works well. Lay your project on a large table or on the floor, depending on the size, shaping and smoothing by hand as much as possible. Adjust your steam iron to the permanent press setting, then hold slightly above the stitches, allowing the steam to penetrate the thread. Do not rest the iron on the item. Gently pull and smooth the stitches into shape, spray lightly with starch and allow to dry completely.

Funtime
Fashions

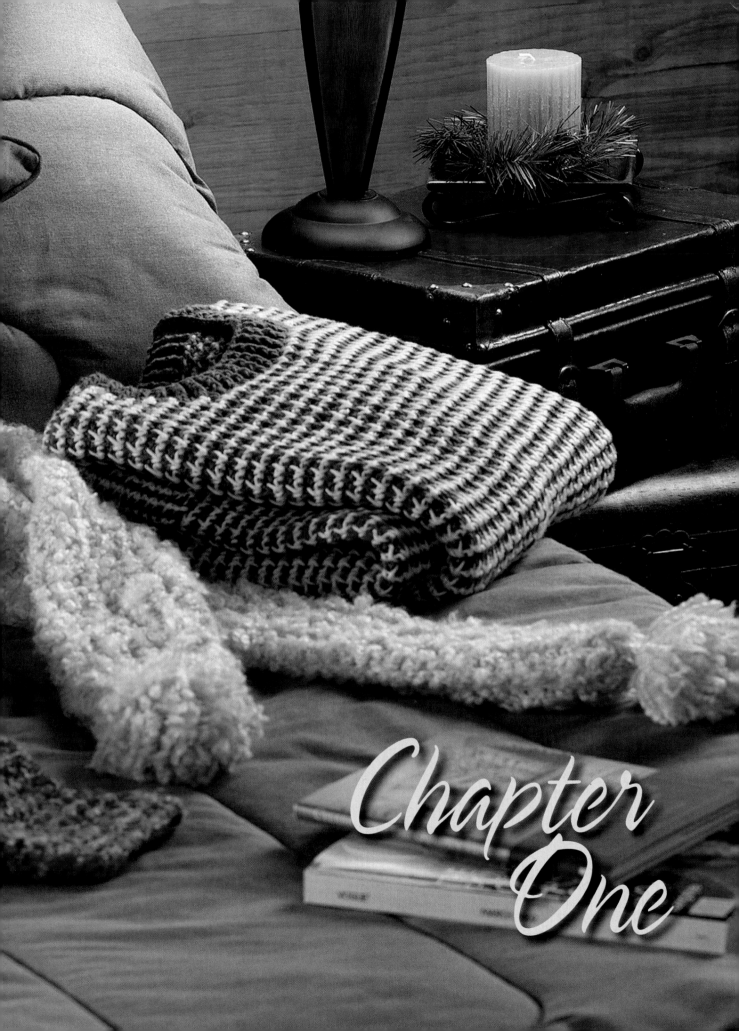

Chapter
One

Jacket Elegance

DESIGNED BY ANN PARNELL

Greet cool weather in style with this classicly chic jacket crocheted in cozy, chunky weight yarn. It works up easily in one piece from sleeve to sleeve, with no assembly required!

FINISHED SIZES: Instructions given fit women's 36" bust (S). Changes for 39" (M), 41" (L) and 46" (XL) busts are in [ ].

MATERIALS: 12 [13, 14, 16] oz. each rose and variegated chunky yarn; tapestry needle; H and H double-ended swivel hooks or hook size needed to obtain gauge.

GAUGE: With **double-ended hook,** 5 pattern sts = 2½"; 6 pattern rows = 1".

NOTES: Read General Instructions on page 6 before beginning pattern.

Use double-ended hook unless otherwise stated.

Jacket is worked in one piece from sleeve to sleeve.

JACKET

Row 1: Starting at bottom of one sleeve, with variegated, ch 35, pull up lp in second ch from hook and in each ch across leaving all lps on hook, turn. *(35 lps on hook)*

Row 2: With rose, yo, pull through one lp on hook, (ch 1, yo, pull through 3 lps on hook) across, **do not turn.**

Row 3: Ch 1, skip first 2 vertical bars, pull up lp in next ch sp, (yo, pull up lp in next ch sp) across to last vertical bar, pull up lp in last vertical bar, turn.

Rows 4-5: With variegated, repeat rows 2 and 3.

Row 6: Repeat row 2.

Row 7: For **increase,** ch 2, pull up lp in second ch from hook, (yo, pull up lp in next ch sp) across to last vertical bar, pull up lp in last vertical bar, turn. *(37 lps on hook)*

Row 8: With variegated, repeat row 2.

Row 9: Repeat row 7. *(39 lps on hook)*

Rows 10-13 [10-13]: For **S and M sizes only,** repeat rows 2-5.

Rows 14-73 [14-73]: For **S and M sizes only,** repeat rows 2-13 consecutively, ending with *59 lps on hook* in last row.

Rows [10-73, 10-73]: For **L and XL bust sizes,** repeat rows 2-9 consecutively, ending with 71 lps on hook in last row.

Rows 74-102: For **all sizes,** repeat rows 2-5 consecutively, ending with row 2. At end of last

continued on page 18

Stars & Stripes Purse

DESIGNED BY ALEXANDRIA HACKER

Show your pride in the red, white and blue wherever you go with this distinctive purse that's both pretty and patriotic!

FINISHED SIZE: 11" square not including Strap.

MATERIALS: Worsted yarn— 8 oz. each red and white, 4 oz. blue; 1¼" x 1½" buckle; tapestry needle; G double-ended and G hooks or hook sizes needed to obtain gauges.

GAUGES: With **G double-ended hook,** 9 sts = 2"; 16 pattern rows = 1". With **G hook,** 9 sc = 2".

NOTES: Read General Instructions on page 6 before beginning pattern.

Use double-ended hook unless otherwise stated.

If using one large skein of red or white, you will need to wind it into two separate balls.

PURSE

Row 1: With red, ch 101, pull up lp in second ch from hook and in each ch across leaving all lps on hook, turn. *(101 lps on hook)*

Row 2: With second skein or ball of red, work lps off hook, **do not turn.**

Row 3: Ch 1, skip first vertical bar, pull up lp under both strands of each **horizontal bar** *(see illustration)* across, turn.

**Horizontal
Bar**

Row 4: With red, work lps off hook, **do not turn.**

Rows 5-16: Repeat rows 3 and 4 alternately. At end of last row, fasten off.

Row 17: Join white with sl st in first vertical bar, ch 1, pull up lp under both strands of each horizontal bar across, turn.

Row 18: With second skein or ball of white, work lps off hook, **do not turn.**

Row 19: Ch 1, skip first vertical bar, pull up lp under both strands of each horizontal bar across, turn.

Rows 20-32: Repeat rows 18 and 19 alternately, ending with row 18. At end of last row, fasten off.

Row 33: Join red with sl st in first vertical bar, ch 1, pull up lp under both strands of each horizontal bar across, turn.

Rows 34-176: Repeat rows 2-33 consecutively, ending with row 16.

Short Strap

Row 1: With red, ch 116, pull up lp in second ch from hook and in each ch across leaving all lps on hook, turn. *(116 lps on hook)*

Row 2: With second skein or ball of red, work lps off hook, **do not turn.**

Row 3: Ch 1, skip first vertical bar, pull up lp under both strands of each horizontal bar across, turn.

Row 4: With red, work lps off hook, **do not turn.**

Rows 5-12: Repeat rows 3 and 4 alternately. At end of last row, fasten off.

Long Strap

With red, ch 151, work same as Short Strap.

Flap

Row 1: With blue, ch 50 *(ch more or less to fit across short edge of Purse),* pull up lp in second ch from hook and in each ch across leaving all lps on hook, turn. *(50 lps on hook)*

Row 2: With second skein or ball of blue, work lps off hook, **do not turn.**

Row 3: Ch 1, skip first vertical bar, pull up lp under both strands of each horizontal bar across, turn.

Rows 4-78: Repeat rows 2 and 3 alternately. At end of last row, fasten off.

Assembly

1: Fold Purse in half crosswise. Sew one end of Short Strap to fold on on one side of Purse forming side of Purse and strap. Sew other Strap other side of Purse in same manner.

2: Holding last row of Flap and back side of Purse wrong sides together, working through both thicknesses, with Flap facing you, with G hook and blue, join with sc in first st, sc in each st across; for **Flap edging,** working on Flap only, evenly spacing sts so piece lays flat, sc across ends of rows; working in starting ch on opposite side of row 1, 3 sc in first ch, sc in each ch across with 3 sc in last ch; evenly spacing sts so piece lays flat, sc across ends of rows, join with sl st in first sc. Fasten off.

3: Wrap red around outer edge of buckle covering completely leaving middle bar uncovered. Secure ends.

4: Sew end of Short Strap to middle bar of buckle covering bar completely. Secure ends. Insert end of Long Strap through buckle; adjust to desired length.

STAR (make 5)

Rnd 1: With G hook and white, ch 2, 10 sc in second ch from hook, join with sl st in first sc. *(10 sc made)*

Rnd 2: Ch 4, sc in second ch from hook, hdc in next ch, dc in last ch, (sl st in next 2 sts of last rnd, ch 4, sc in second ch from hook, hdc in next ch, dc in last ch) 4 times, sl st in last st of last rnd, join with sl st in joining sl st of last rnd. Fasten off.

Sew Stars evenly spaced across Flap as shown in photo.♦

Jacket Elegance

continued from page 15

row, ch 50, pull up long lp to be picked up later. Join a separate strand of rose in other end of last row, ch 50, fasten off.

Row 103: For **body of Jacket,** pick up dropped lp, pull up lp in second ch from hook, pull up lp in next 48 chs, pull up lp in first 2 vertical bars of sleeve, (yo, pull up lp in next ch sp) across to last vertical bar, pull up lp in last vertical bar, pull up lp in next 50 chs, turn. *(159 lps on hook) [159 lps on hook, 171 lps on hook, 171 lps on hook]*

Rows 104-105: Repeat rows 4 and 5.

Rows 106-142 [106-146, 106-150, 106-158]: Repeat rows 2-5 consecutively, ending with row 2.

Row 143 [147, 151, 159]: For **back neck shaping,** ch 1, skip first 2 vertical bars, pull up lp in next ch sp, (yo, pull up lp in next ch sp) 38 [38, 41, 41] times, pull up lp in next 2 vertical bars at same time leaving remaining sts unworked forming first front section, turn. *(79 [79, 85, 85] lps on hook)*

Rows 144-145 [148-149, 152-153, 160-161]: Repeat rows 4 and 5.

Rows 146-182 [150-186, 154-190, 162-198]: Repeat rows 2-5 consecutively, ending with row 2. At end of last row, pull up long lp to be picked up later. Join a separate strand of rose in last st at other end of row, ch 80 [80, 86, 86] forming second front section, fasten off.

Row 183 [187, 191, 199]: Pick up dropped lp at beginning of row, ch 1, skip first 2 vertical bars, pull up lp in next ch sp, (yo, pull up lp in next ch sp) across to last vertical bar, pull up lp in last vertical bar, pull up lp in next 80 [80, 86, 86] chs, turn. *(159 lps on hook) [159 lps on hook, 171 lps on hook, 171 lps on hook]*

Rows 184-185 [188-189, 192-193, 200-201]: Repeat rows 4 and 5.

Rows 186-222 [190-230, 194-238, 202-254]: Repeat rows 2-5 consecutively, ending with row 2. At end of last row, fasten off.

Row 223 [231, 239, 255]: For **second sleeve,** join rose with sl st in 25th ch sp, (yo, pull up lp in next ch sp) 29 [29, 35, 35] times leaving remaining ch sps unworked, turn. *(59 lps on hook) [59 lps on hook, 71 lps on hook, 71 lps on hook]*

Rows 224-225 [232-233, 240-241, 256-257]: Repeat rows 4 and 5.

Rows 226-254 [234-262, 242-270, 258-286]: Repeat rows 2-5 consecutively, ending with row 2.

Row 255 [263, 271, 287]: Ch 1, skip first 2 vertical bars; for **decrease,** (pull up lp in next ch sp) 3 times; (yo, pull up lp in next ch sp) across to last vertical bar, pull up lp in last vertical bar, turn. *(57 lps on hook) [57 lps on hook, 69 lps on hook, 69 lps on hook]*

Row 256 [264, 272, 288]: Repeat row 4.

Row 257 [265, 273, 289]: Repeat row 255 [263, 271, 287]. *(55 lps on hook) [55 lps on hook, 67 lps on hook, 67 lps on hook]*

Rows 258-265 [266-273, 274-277, 290-293]: Repeat rows 2-5 consecutively.

Row 266 [274, 278, 294]: Repeat row 2.

Rows 267-269 [275-277, 279-281, 295-297]: Repeat row 255 [263, 271, 287] and row 4 alternately, ending with row 255 [263, 271, 287] and *51 [51, 63, 63] lps on hook* in last row.

Rows 270-277 [278-285, 282-285, 298-301]: Repeat rows 2-5 consecutively.

Rows 278-323 [286-331, 286-339, 302-355]: Repeat rows 266-277 [274-285, 278-285, 294-301] consecutively, ending with row 275 [283, 283, 299] and *35 lps on hook* in last row.

Row 324 [332, 340, 356]: With variegated, ch 1, skip first 2 vertical bars, sl st in next ch sp, (ch 1, sl st in next ch sp) across to last vertical bar, sl st in last vertical bar. Fasten off.

Sew sleeve/side seams, leaving 5" unsewn on bottom of each side for slit.

FRONT BAND

Row 1: Working across front and neck of Jacket, join variegated with sl st in first st at bottom of Jacket, ch 1, pull up lp in each st across first front; working in ends of rows, pull up lp in each "stripe" across neck, pull up lp in each st across second front, turn.

Row 2: With rose, pull through one lp on hook, (yo, pull through 2 lps on hook) across, **do not turn.**

Row 3: Ch 1, skip first vertical bar, pull up lp in top strand of each **horizontal bar** *(see illustration)* across, turn.

Horizontal Bar

Row 4: With variegated, repeat row 2.

Row 5: Ch 1, skip first vertical bar, pull up lp in top strand of each horizontal bar across, turn.

Rows 6-26: Repeat rows 2-5 consecutively, ending with row 2. At end of last row, fasten off.

EDGING

For **bottom edging,** with predominantly variegated side facing you, working in ends of rows and in sts across bottom of Jacket, evenly spacing sts so piece lays flat, with H hook and variegated, join with sc in last row on Front Band, sc across bottom of Jacket including slit edges across to opposite corner with 3 sc in each corner of slits. Fasten off.

For **sleeve edging,** with predominantly variegated side facing you, working around bottom edge of sleeve, with H hook and variegated, join with sc in sleeve seam, sc evenly spaced around sleeve, join with sl st in first sc. Fasten off. Repeat around other sleeve.♦

Shell Vest

DESIGNED BY ANN PARNELL

Vests are always in vogue no matter what the style. The pretty shell stitch pattern in this classic design works up doubly quick with bulky yarn and large-size hook.

FINISHED SIZES: Instructions given fit women's 36" bust. Changes for 40", 44" and 48" busts are in [ ].

MATERIALS: 14 [16, 18, 20] oz. tan bulky yarn; 7 [8, 9, 10] oz. green 100 percent cotton worsted yarn; tapestry needle; I and K double-ended hooks or hook sizes needed to obtain gauges.

GAUGES: With **double-ended hook and bulky or worsted yarn,** 5 shells = 4½"; 4 rows worked in pattern = 1". With **I hook and bulky yarn,** 5 sts = 2".

SPECIAL STITCH: For **shell,** yo, pull through 4 lps on hook.

NOTES: Read General Instructions on page 6 before beginning pattern.

Use double-ended hook unless otherwise stated.

BACK

Row 1: With tan, ch 66 [72, 78, 84], pull up lp in second ch from hook and in each ch across leaving all lps on hook, turn. *(66 lps on hook) [72 lps on hook, 78 lps on hook, 84 lps on hook]*

Row 2: With green, pull through one lp on hook, ch 2, *shell *(see Special Stitch),* ch 3; repeat from * across to last 3 lps on hook, yo, pull through last 3 lps on hook *(shell),* **do not turn.** *(22 shells) [24 shells, 26 shells, 28 shells]*

Row 3: Ch 1, skipping shells, pull up lp in **back lp** *(see Stitch Guide)* of each ch across, turn. *(66 lps) [72 lps, 78 lps, 84 lps]*

Rows 4-5: With tan, repeat rows 2-3.

Rows 6-93: Repeat rows 2-5 consecutively.

Row 94: For **first armhole shaping,** with green, pull through one lp on hook, ch 1, (shell, ch 2) 3 [4, 4, 5] times, (shell, ch 3) across to last 3 lps on hook, yo, pull through last 3 lps on hook, **do not turn.** *(22 shells) [24 shells, 26 shells, 28 shells]*

Row 95: For **second armhole shaping,** ch 1, working over tan *(carry across back of work),* sc in **back lp** of next 9 [12, 12, 15] chs; drop tan, pull up lp in next 47 [47, 53, 53] chs leaving remaining chs unworked, turn. *(48 lps on hook)*

continued on page 29

Twilight Slippers

DESIGNED BY DEBBIE TABOR

Relax in cozy comfort with fancy footwear worked in soft, chunky yarn that's a treat for your feet!

FINISHED SIZE: Fits up to 12" sole.

MATERIALS: 2 oz. variegated chunky yarn; 2 oz. plum worsted yarn; tapestry needle; J double-ended hook or hook size needed to obtain gauge.

GAUGE: 4 sts = 1"; 6 pattern rows = 1".

NOTE: Read General Instructions on page 6 before beginning pattern.

SLIPPER (make 2)
Sole

Row 1: With plum, ch 27, pull up lp in second ch from hook and in each ch across leaving all lps on hook, turn. *(27 lps on hook)*

Row 2: With variegated, work lps off hook, **do not turn.**

Row 3: Ch 1, skip first vertical bar, pull up lp in top strand of next 2 **horizontal bars** *(see illustration)*, (pull up lp in next 3 vertical bars at same time, pull up lp in top strand of next horizontal bar, pull up lp in next vertical bar, pull up lp in top strand of next horizontal bar) across, turn.

Horizontal Bar

Row 4: With plum, work lps off hook, **do not turn.**

Row 5: Repeat row 3.

Rows 6-24: Repeat rows 2-5 consecutively, ending with row 4.

Row 25: Ch 1, skip first vertical bar, pull up lp in top strand of each horizontal bar across, turn.

Row 26: With variegated, work lps off hook, **do not turn.**

Row 27: Ch 1, skip first vertical bar, pull up lp in top strand of each horizontal bar across, turn.

Row 28: With plum, work lps off hook, **do not turn.**

Rows 29-36: Repeat rows 25-28 consecutively.

Row 37: Repeat row 3.

Rows 38-64: Repeat rows 2-5 consecutively, ending with row 4. At end of last row, leaving long plum end for sewing, fasten off both colors.

For **toe,** thread plum yarn through sts of last row, pull tight to gather, secure. For **heel seam,** fold row 1 in half, matching sts, sew together.

Vamp

Row 1: With plum, ch 23, pull up lp in second ch from hook and in each ch across leaving all lps on hook, turn. *(23 lps on hook)*

Row 2: With variegated, work lps off hook, **do not turn.**

Row 3: Ch 1, skip first vertical bar, pull up lp in top strand of each horizontal bar across, turn.

Row 4: With plum, work lps off hook, **do not turn.**

Row 5: Ch 1, skip first vertical bar, pull up lp in top strand of each horizontal bar across, turn.

Rows 6-36: Repeat rows 2-5 consecutively, ending with row 4. At end of last row, leaving long plum end for sewing, fasten off.

For **toe,** weave plum through ends of rows on one end, pull tight to gather, secure.

Cuff

Row 1: With plum, ch 6, pull up lp in second ch from hook and in each ch across leaving all lps on hook, turn. *(6 lps on hook)*

Row 2: With variegated, work lps off hook, **do not turn.**

Row 3: Ch 1, skip first vertical bar, pull up lp under both strands of each horizontal bar across, turn.

Row 4: With plum, work lps off hook, **do not turn.**

Row 5: Ch 1, skip first vertical bar, pull up

continued on page 29

Cross-Stitch Vest

DESIGNED BY MARGRET WILLSON

An eye-catching striped design creates the flair in this smartly-fashioned vest. One-piece styling and swivel hook technique combine to make this design a fast-and-fun addition to any casual wardrobe!

FINISHED SIZE: Instructions given fit women's 34" bust *(Small)*. Changes for 39" *(Medium)* and 44" *(Large)* busts are in [ ].

MATERIALS: Worsted yarn— 12 [13, 14] oz. rose and 8 [9, 10] oz. aran; tapestry needle; G double-ended swivel and G hooks or hook sizes needed to obtain gauges.

GAUGES: With **double-ended hook,** 4 dc lps = 1"; 8 pattern rows = 2". With **G hook,** 4 sts = 1".

SPECIAL STITCHES: For **dc knit (dc K),** yo, insert hook between front and back vertical bars and under horizontal bar of next st *(see illustration)* yo, pull lp through, yo, pull through 2 lps on hook.

For **ending decrease (end dec),** yo, pull through 2 lps on hook.

For **beginning decrease (beg dec),** dc k in next vertical bar, yo, pull through 2 lps on hook.

To **dc next 3 sts tog,** (yo, insert hook in next st, yo, pull through 2 lps on hook) 3 times, yo, pull through all 4 lps on hook.

NOTES: Read General Instructions on page 6 before beginning pattern.

Use double-ended hook unless otherwise stated.

Vest is worked in one piece to underarms.

VEST

Row 1: With aran, ch 146 [164, 184], pull up lp in second ch from hook and in each ch across leaving all lps on hook, turn. *(146 lps on hook) [164 lps on hook, 184 lps on hook]*

Row 2: With rose, work lps off hook, **do not turn.**

Row 3: Ch 1, skip first vertical bar, **dc K** *(see Special Stitches)* across, turn.

Row 4: With aran, work lps off hook, **do not turn.**

Row 5: Ch 1, skip first vertical bar; for **cross stitch (cr st),** skip next vertical bar, pull up lp in

continued on page 30

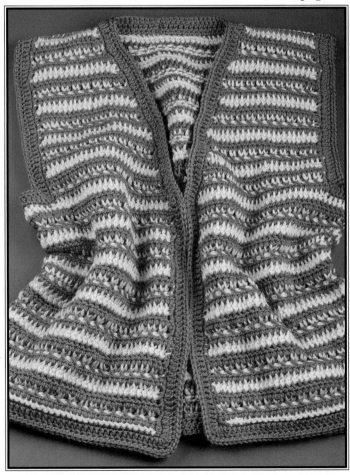

Tri-Color Dog Sweater

Designed by Darla Fanton

Give your canine friend two trendy looks in one with his own chic, reversible sweater!

FINISHED SIZES: Instructions given fit dog measuring 15" long from shoulder to rear and up to 23" girth (S). Changes for 18" long/25" girth (M) and 21" long/27" girth (L) are in [ ].

MATERIALS: Sport yarn— 2½ oz. navy #853, 2 oz. maroon and 1½ oz. off-white; 8 off-white ¾" flat buttons; tapestry needle; G and H double-ended hooks or hook sizes needed to obtain gauges.

GAUGES: With **double-ended hook,** 7 pattern sts = 3"; 8 pattern rows = 1". With **G hook,** 4 sc = 1".

SPECIAL STITCH: For **cast on,** wrap yarn around thumb *(see illustration 1),* insert hook from front to back through loop. Remove thumb from loop and pull yarn around hook *(see illustration 2).*

Cast On

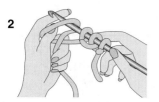

NOTES: Read General Instructions on page 6 before beginning pattern.

Use double-ended hook unless otherwise stated.

SWEATER

Row 1: With navy, ch 32 [40, 48], pull up lp in second ch from hook and in each ch across leaving all lps on hook, turn. *(32 ps on hook) [40 lps on hook, 48 lps on hook]*

Row 2: With off-white, pull through first 2 lps on hook, (ch 1, yo, pull through 3 lps on hook) across, **do not turn.**

Row 3: Ch 1, pull up lp in first vertical bar,

yo, pull up lp in second vertical bar, (yo, skip next ch sp, pull up lp in next 2 vertical bars at same time) across to last 2 vertical bars, (yo, pull up lp in next vertical bar) 2 times, turn. *(36 lps on hook)* *[44 lps on hook, 52 lps on hook]*

Row 4: With maroon, repeat row 2.

Row 5: Repeat row 3. *(40 lps on hook)* *[48 lps on hook, 56 lps on hook]*

Rows 6-7: With navy, repeat rows 2 and 3. *(44 lps on hook)* *[52 lps on hook, 60 lps on hook]*

Rows 8-9: Repeat rows 2 and 3. *(48 lps on hook)* *[56 lps on hook, 64 lps on hook]*

Row 10: With maroon, repeat row 2.

Rows 11-19: Repeat rows 5-10 consecutively, ending with row 7 and *68 [76, 84] lps on hook* in last row.

Row 20: Repeat row 2.

Row 21: Ch 1, pull up lp in first 2 vertical bars at same time, (yo, pull up lp in next 2 vertical bars at same time) across, turn.

Rows 22-60 [22-72, 22-84]: Working in color sequence of maroon, navy and off-white, repeat rows 20 and 21 alternately, ending with row 20 and navy in last row. At end of last row, fasten off maroon.

Row 61 [73, 85]: Ch 1, pull up lp in first 2 vertical bars at same time, (yo, pull up lp in next 2 vertical bars at same time) across; for **tummy band, cast on** 42 lps *(see Special Stitch)*, turn. *(110 lps on hook)* *[118 lps on hook, 126 lps on hook]*

Rows 62-84 [74-96, 86-108]: Working in color sequence of off-white, maroon and navy, repeat rows 20 and 21 alternately, ending with row 20 and navy.

Row 85 [97, 109]: Ch 1, pull up lp in first 2 vertical bars at same time, (yo, pull up lp in next 2 vertical bars at same time) 33 [37, 41] times leaving remaining vertical bars unworked, turn. *(68 lps on hook)* *[76 lps on hook, 84 lps on hook]*

Row 86-120 [98-144, 110-168]: Working in color sequence of off-white, maroon and navy, repeat rows 20 and 21 alternately, ending with row 20 and navy.

Row 121 [145, 169]: For **first front extension,** ch 1, pull up lp in first 2 vertical bars at same time, (yo, pull up lp in next 2 vertical bars at same time) 4 [5, 6] times leaving remaining vertical bars unworked, turn. *(10 lps on hook)* *[12 lps on hook, 14 lps on hook]*

Rows 122-168 [146-192, 170-216]: Working in color sequence of off-white, maroon and navy, repeat rows 20 and 21 alternately, ending with row 20 and navy. At end of last row, fasten off.

Row 121 [145, 169]: For **second front extension,** with predominantly off-white side facing you, skip next 24 [26, 28] pair of unworked vertical bars on row 120 [144, 168], with navy, pull up lp in next 2 vertical bars at same time, (yo, pull up lp in next 2 vertical bars at same time) 4 [5, 6] times, turn *(10 lps on hook)* *[12 lps on hook, 14 lps on hook]*

Rows 122-168 [146-192, 17-216]: Repeat same rows of first front extension, **do not fasten off.**

EDGING

Rnd 1: With predominantly navy/maroon side facing you, evenly spacing sts so piece lays flat, with G hook and navy, ch 1, sc in each st and in end of each row around with 3 sc in each corner, join with sl st in first sc.

Rnd 2: Ch 1, sc in each st around, join. Fasten off.

FINISHING

With navy/maroon side facing you, sew one button centered 1" from short end of first front extension. Sew a second button centered to same extension 4" from first button. Spaces between sts on second extension will be used as buttonholes.

Sew two buttons to off-white side of Sweater underneath first two buttons.

With navy/maroon side facing you, sew two buttons spaced 3" apart to body of Sweater opposite tummy band using sp between sts on tummy band as buttonholes.

Sew remaining two buttons to off-white side of Sweater opposite previous two buttons.♦

Twilight Slippers

continued from page 23

lp under both strands of each horizontal bar across, turn.

Rows 6-52: Repeat rows 2-5 consecutively, ending with row 4. At end of last row, fasten off both colors.

Assembly

Matching toes, sew sides of Sole and Vamp together leaving 1" on each side of Vamp unsewn. Easing to fit, sew ends and one long edge of Cuff to the 1" of Vamp left unsewn and to remainder of Sole sides.♦

Shell Vest

continued from page 21

[48 lps on hook, 54 lps on hook, 54 lps on hook]

Row 96: With tan, pull through first 4 lps on hook, ch 2, (shell, ch 3) across to last 6 lps on hook, yo, pull through last 6 lps on hook, **do not turn.** *(15 shells) [15 shells, 17 shells, 17 shells]*

Row 97: Ch 1, skipping shells, pull up lp in **back lp** of each ch across, turn. *(42 lps on hook) [42 lps on hook, 48 lps on hook, 48 lps on hook]*

Rows 98-129: Repeat rows 2-5 consecutively.

Row 130: With green, pull through one lp on hook, ch 1, (shell, ch 2) across to last 3 lps on hook, yo, pull through last 3 lps on hook. Fasten off.

FIRST FRONT

Row 1: With tan, ch 33 [36, 39, 42], pull up lp in second ch from hook and in each ch across leaving all lps on hook, turn. *(33 lps on hook) [36 lop on hook, 39 lps on hook, 42 lps on hook]*

Rows 2-91: Repeat rows 2-5 of Back consecutively, ending with row 3.

Row 92: For **front shaping,** with tan, pull through first 4 lps on hook, ch 2, (shell, ch 3) across to last 3 lps on hook, yo, pull through last 3 lps on hook, **do not turn.** *(11 shells) [12 shells, 13 shells, 14 shells]*

Row 93: Ch 1, skipping shells, pull up lp in **back lp** of each ch across, turn. *(30 lps on hook) [33 lps on hook, 36 lps on hook, 39 lps on hook]*

Row 94: For **armhole shaping,** with green, pull through one lp on hook, ch 1, (shell, ch 2) 3 [4, 4, 5] times, (shell, ch 3) across to last 3 lps on hook, yo, pull through last 3 lps on hook, **do not turn.**

Row 95: Ch 1, skipping shells, pull up lp in next 20 [20, 23, 23] chs leaving remaining chs unworked for armhole, turn. *(21 lps on hook) [21 lps on hook, 24 lps on hook, 24 lop on hook]*

Rows 96-97: Repeat rows 4 and 5 of Back.

Rows 98-99: With green, repeat rows 92 and 93, ending with *18 [18, 21, 21] lps on hook* in last row.

Rows 100-101: Repeat rows 92 and 93, ending with *15 [15, 18, 18] lps on hook* in last row.

Rows 102-107: Repeat rows 2-5 of Back consecutively, ending with row 3.

Rows 108-109: Repeat rows 92 and 93, ending with *12 [12, 15, 15] lps on hook* in last row.

Rows 110-129: Repeat rows 2-5 of Back consecutively.

Row 130: With green, pull through one lp on hook, ch 1, (shell, ch 2) across to last 3 lps on hook, yo, pull through last 3 lps on hook. Fasten off.

SECOND FRONT

Row 1: With tan, ch 33 [36, 39, 42], pull up lp in second ch from hook and in each ch across leaving all lps on hook, turn. *(33 lps on hook) [36 lps on hook, 39 lps on hook, 42 lps on hook]*

Rows 2-91: Repeat rows 2-5 of Back consecutively, ending with row 3.

Row 92: For **front shaping,** with tan, pull through one lp on hook, ch 2, (shell, ch 3) across to last 6 lps on hook, yo, pull through last 6 lps on hook, **do not turn.** *(10 shells) [11 shells, 12 shells, 13 shells]*

Row 93: Ch 1, skipping shells, pull up lp in **back lp** of each ch across, turn. *(30 lps on hook) [33 lps on hook, 36 lps on hook, 39 lps on hook]*

Row 94: With green, pull through one lp on

hook, ch 2, (shell, ch 3) across to last 3 lps on hook, yo, pull through last 3 lps on hook, **do not turn.**

Row 95: For **armhole shaping,** ch 1, working over tan *(carry across back of work),* sc in **back lp** of next 9 [12, 12, 15] chs; drop tan, pull up lp in each ch across, **do not turn.** *(21 lps on hook) [21 lps on hook, 24 lps on hook, 24 lps on hook]*

Rows 96-97: Repeat rows 4 and 5 of Back.

Rows 98-99: With green, repeat rows 2 and 3 of Back.

Row 100: With tan, pull through first 4 lps on hook, ch 2, (shell, ch 3) across to last 6 lps on hook, yo, pull through last 6 lps on hook, **do not turn.**

Row 101: Repeat row 5 of Back.

Rows 102-107: Repeat rows 2-5 of Back consecutively, ending with row 3.

Rows 108-109: Repeat rows 92 and 93, ending with *12 [12, 15, 15] lps on hook* in last row.

Rows 110-129: Repeat rows 2-5 of Back consecutively.

Row 130: With green, pull through one lp on hook, ch 1, (shell, ch 2) across to last 3 lps on hook, yo, pull through last 3 lps on hook. Fasten off.

For **shoulder seams,** sew last row of each Front to corresponding sts on last row of Back, being sure to match armhole shapings of Fronts and Back.

Sew **side seams,** leaving rows 1-31 unsewn for side slits.

For **outer edging,** with predominantly tan side of Vest facing you, using I hook and tan, evenly spacing sts so piece lays flat, join with sc in bottom corner of one Front, sc across bottom of Vest and hdc in ends of rows of each slit and around front of Vest with 3 hdc in each corner, join with sl st in first sc. Fasten off.

For **armhole edging,** with predominantly tan side of Vest facing you, using I hook and tan, evenly spacing sts so piece lays flat, join with sl st in any underarm st, ch 2 *(counts as first hdc),* hdc around armhole, join with sl st in top of ch-2. Fasten off. Repeat around other armhole.♦

Cross-Stitch Vest

continued from page 25

next vertical bar, pull up lp in last skipped vertical bar; cr st across to last vertical bar, pull up lp in last vertical bar, turn.

Row 6: With rose, work lps off hook, **do not turn.**

Row 7: Ch 1, skip first vertical bar, dc K across, turn.

Row 8: With aran, work lps off hook, **do not turn.**

Row 9: Ch 1, skip first vertical bar, dc K across, turn.

Rows 10-50 [10-58, 10-58]: Repeat rows 2-9 consecutively, ending with row 2.

Row 51 [59, 59]: For **first front,** ch 1, skip first vertical bar, dc K 29 [33, 37] times leaving remaining sts unworked, turn. *(30 lps on hook) [34 lps on hook, 38 lps on hook]*

Row 52 [60, 60]: With aran, work lps off hook, **do not turn.**

Row 53 [61, 61]: Repeat row 5.

Row 54 [62, 62]: With rose, work lps off hook, **do not turn.**

Note: Decreases form neck shaping on front.

Row 55 [63, 63]: Ch 1, skip first vertical bar; for **beginning decrease (beg dec),** dc K in next vertical bar, yo, pull through 2 lps on hook; dc K across, turn. *(29 lps on hook) [33 lps on hook, 37 lps on hook]*

Row 56 [64, 64]: With aran, work lps off hook, **do not turn.**

Row 57 [65, 65]: Ch 1, skip first vertical bar, dc K across; **end dec** *(see Special Stitches),* turn. *(28 lps on hook) [32 lps on hook, 36 lps on hook]*

Row 58 [66, 66]: With rose, work lps off hook, **do not turn.**

Row 59 [67, 67]: Ch 1, skip first vertical bar, beg dec, dc K across, turn. *(27 lps on hook) [31 lps on hook, 35 lps on hook]*

Row 60 [68, 68]: With aran, work lps off hook, **do not turn.**

Row 61 [69, 69]: Ch 1, skip first vertical bar, cr st across, turn.

Row 62 [70, 70]: With rose, work lps off hook, **do not turn.**

Row 63 [71, 71]: Repeat row 59 [67, 67]. *(26 lps on hook) [30 lps on hook, 34 lps on hook]*

Row 64 [72, 72]: With aran, work lps off hook, **do not turn.**

Row 65 [73, 73]: Ch 1, skip first vertical bar, dc K across, end dec, turn. *(25 lps on hook) [29 lps on hook, 33 lps on hook]*

Row 66 [74, 74]: With rose, work lps off hook, **do not turn.**

Row 67 [75, 75]: Repeat row 59 [67, 67]. *(24 lps on hook) [28 lps on hook, 32 lps on hook]*

Row 68 [76, 76]: With aran, work lps off hook, **do not turn.**

Row 69 [77, 77]: Ch 1, skip first vertical bar, cr st across to last vertical bar, pull up lp in last vertical bar, turn.

Row 70 [78, 78]: With rose, work lps off hook, **do not turn.**

Row 71 [79, 79]: Repeat row 59 [67, 67]. *(23 lps on hook) [27 lps on hook, 31 lps on hook]*

Row 72 [80, 80]: With aran, work lps off hook, **do not turn.**

Row 73 [81, 81]: Repeat row 65 [73, 73]. *(22 lps on hook) [26 lps on hook, 30 lps on hook]*

Rows 74-95 [82-103, 82-97]: Repeat rows 58-73 [66-81, 66-81] consecutively, ending with row 63 [71, 81] and *14 [18, 24] lps on hook* in last row.

Rows [98-103]: For **large only,** repeat rows 2-7.

Row 96 [104, 104]: For **all sizes,** ch 1, sl st in each vertical bar across. Fasten off.

Row 51 [59, 59]: For **armhole,** with rose, sl st in next 15 [15, 17] unworked vertical bars of row 50 [58, 58]; for **back,** ch 1, dc K in next 57 [67, 75] vertical bars leaving remaining sts unworked, turn. *(58 lps on hook) [68 lps on hook, 76 lps on hook]*

Rows 52-57 [60-65, 60-65]: Repeat rows 4-9.

Rows 58-95 [66-103, 66-103]: Repeat rows 2-9 consecutively, ending with row 7.

Row 96 [104, 104]: Ch 1, sl st in each vertical bar across. Fasten off.

Row 51 [59, 59]: For **armhole,** with rose, sl st in next 15 [15, 17] unworked vertical bars of row 50 [58, 58]; for **second front,** ch 1, dc K in last 29 [33, 37] vertical bars, turn. *(30 lps on hook) [34 lps on hook, 38 lps on hook]*

Rows 52-96 [60-104, 60-104]: Repeat same rows of first front, reversing beg and end decreases.

Sew shoulder seams.

Armhole

Rnd 1: Working in ends of rows and in sts around one armhole, evenly spacing sts so piece lays flat, with G hook and rose, join with sc in center of underarm, sc around, join with sl st in first sc.

Rnd 2: Ch 3 *(counts as first dc),* dc in each st around with **dc next 3 sts tog** *(see Special Stitches)* at each corner of underarm, join with sl st in top of ch-3.

Rnd 3: Ch 1, sc in each st around with sc next 2 sts tog at each corner of underarm, join with sl st in first sc. Fasten off.

Repeat around other armhole.

Edging

Rnd 1: Working in ends of rows and in sts around entire Vest, evenly spacing sts so piece lays flat, with G hook, join rose with sc in center back of neck, sc around with 3 sc in each bottom corner, join with sl st in first sc.

Rnd 2: Ch 3, dc in each st around with dc next 3 sts tog at each shoulder seam, 2 dc at base of each neck shaping *(row 49 [57, 57])* and 5 dc in center st of each bottom corner, join with sl st in top of ch-3.

Rnd 3: Ch 1, sc in each st around with (sc next 2 sts tog) at each shoulder seam, 2 sc at base of each neck shaping and 3 sc in center st of each bottom corner, join with sl st in first sc. Fasten off.♦

Guys 'n' Gals Sweater

Designed by Margret Willson

Whether worn by a man or a woman, this handsomely styled pullover, stitched in soft, fuzzy worsted yarn, is a must-have for chilly days!

FINISHED SIZE: Instructions given fit 36" chest/bust *(small)*. Changes for 40" *(medium)*, 44" *(large)* and 48" *(x-large)* chest/bust sizes are in [ ].

MATERIALS: Fuzzy worsted yarn— 15 [16½, 18, 19½] oz. gray and 13 [14, 15, 16½] oz. off-white; tapestry needle; K double-ended and I hooks or hook sizes needed to obtain gauges.

GAUGES: With **K double-ended hook,** 14 sts = 4"; 28 pattern rows = 4". With **I hook,** 4 sts = 1"; 5 post st rows = 2".

SPECIAL STITCHES: For **knit (K),** insert hook between front and back vertical bars and under horizontal bar of next st *(see illustration)* yo, draw lp through.

For **decrease (dec),** pull up lp in next 2 vertical bars at same time.

For **increase (inc),** K in next vertical bar, pull up in same vertical bar.

NOTES: Read General Instructions on page 6 before beginning pattern.

Use double-ended hook unless otherwise stated.

BACK
Ribbing
Row 1: With I hook and gray, ch 73 [79, 87, 95], dc in fourth ch from hook and in each ch across, turn. *(71 dc made)* [*77 dc made, 85 dc made, 93 dc made*]

Row 2: Ch 3 *(counts as first st),* **dc bp** *(see page 160)* around next st, ***dc fp** *(see page 160)* around next st, dc bp around next st; repeat from * across to last st, dc in last st, turn.

Row 3: Ch 3, dc fp around next st, (dc bp around next st, dc fp around next st) across to last st, dc in last st, turn.

Rows 4-6: Repeat rows 2 and 3 alternately, ending with row 2. At end of last row, change to double-ended hook.

Body
Row 1: Ch 1 *(counts as first st),* pull up lp in

each st across leaving all lps on hook, turn. *(71 lps on hook) [77 lps on hook, 85 lps on hook, 93 lps on hook]*

Row 2: With off-white, work lps off hook, **do not turn.**

Row 3: Ch 1, skip first vertical bar, yo, skip next vertical bar, **K** *(see Special Stitches)* in next vertical bar, (yo, skip next vertical bar, K in next vertical bar) across, turn.

Row 4: With gray, work lps off hook, **do not turn.**

Row 5: Ch 1, skip first vertical bar, pull up lp in each vertical bar across, turn.

Row 6: With off-white, work lps off hook, **do not turn.**

Row 7: Ch 1, skip first vertical bar, (yo, skip next vertical bar, K in next vertical bar) across, turn.

Rows 8-164 [168, 172, 176]: Repeat rows 4-7 consecutively, ending with row 4.

Row 165 [169, 173, 177]: Ch 1, sl st in each vertical bar across. Fasten off.

FRONT
Ribbing
Work same as Back Ribbing.

Body
Rows 1-136 [1-140, 1-144, 1-148]: Repeat same rows of Back Body, ending with row 4.

Row 137 [141, 145, 149]: For **first shoulder,** ch 1, skip first vertical bar, pull up lp in next 26 [28, 30, 34] vertical bars leaving remaining sts unworked, turn. *(27 lps on hook) [29 lps on hook, 31 lps on hook, 35 lps on hook]*

Row 138 [142, 146, 150]: With off-white, work lps off hook, **do not turn.**

Row 139 [143, 147, 151]: Ch 1, skip first vertical bar, (yo, skip next vertical bar, K in next vertical bar) across, turn.

Row 140 [144, 148, 152]: With gray, work lps off hook, **do not turn.**

Row 141 [145, 149, 153]: Ch 1, skip first vertical bar, pull up lp in each vertical bar across to last 2 vertical bars; **dec** *(see Special Stitches)*, turn. *(26 lps on hook) [28 lps on hook, 30 lps on hook, 34 lps on hook]*

Row 142 [146, 150, 154]: With off-white, work lps off hook, **do not turn.**

Row 143 [147, 151, 155]: Ch 1, skip first ver-
tical bar, (yo, skip next vertical bar, K in next vertical bar) across to last vertical bar, pull up lp in last vertical bar, turn.

Row 144 [148, 152, 156]: With gray, work lps off hook, **do not turn.**

Row 145 [149, 153, 157]: Repeat row 141 [145, 149, 153]. *(25 lps on hook) [27 lps on hook, 29 lps on hook, 33 lps on hook]*

Rows 146-163 [150-167, 154-171, 158-175]: Repeat rows 138-145 [142-149, 146-153, 150-157] consecutively, ending with row 139 [143, 147, 151] and *21 [23, 25, 39] lps* on hook.

Row 164 [168, 172, 176]: With gray, work lps off hook, **do not turn.**

Row 165 [169, 173, 177]: Ch 1, sl st in each vertical bar across. Fasten off.

Row 137 [141, 145, 149]: For **neck shaping,** join gray with sl st in next unworked vertical bar, sl st in next 17 [19, 23, 23] vertical bars; for **second shoulder,** ch 1, pull up lp in last 26 [28, 30, 34] sts leaving remaining sts unworked, turn. *(27 lps on hook) [29 lps on hook, 31 lps on hook, 35 lps on hook]*

Row 138 [142, 146, 150]: With off-white, work lps off hook, **do not turn.**

Row 139 [143, 147, 151]: Ch 1, skip first vertical bar, (yo, skip next vertical bar, K in next vertical bar) across, turn.

Row 140 [144, 148, 152]: With gray, work lps off hook, **do not turn.**

Row 141 [145, 149, 153]: Ch 1, skip first vertical bar draw up lp in next vertical bar, dec, pull up lp in each vertical bar across, turn. *(26 lps on hook) [28 lps on hook, 30 lps on hook, 34 lps on hook]*

Row 142 [146, 150, 154]: With off-white, work lps off hook, **do not turn.**

Row 143 [147, 151, 155]: Ch 1, skip first vertical bar, (yo, skip next vertical bar, K in next vertical bar) across to last vertical bar, pull up lp in last vertical bar, turn.

Row 144 [148, 152, 156]: With gray, work lps off hook, **do not turn.**

Row 145 [149, 153, 157]: Repeat row 141 [145, 149, 153]. *(25 lps on hook) [27 lps on hook, 29 lps on hook, 33 lps on hook]*

Rows 146-163 [150-167, 154-171, 158-175]: Repeat rows 138-145 [142-149, 146-153, 150-157] consecutively, ending with row 139 [143,

147, 151] and *21 [23, 25, 29] lps* on hook.

Row 164 [168, 172, 176]: With gray, work lps off hook, **do not turn.**

Row 165 [169, 173, 177]: Ch 1, sl st in each vertical bar across. Fasten off.

Holding Front and Back wrong sides together, sew shoulder seams.

SLEEVE (make 2)
Ribbing

Row 1: With I hook and gray, ch 37 [39, 41, 45], dc in fourth ch from hook and in each ch across, turn. *(35 dc made) [37 dc made, 39 dc made, 43 dc made]*

Row 2: Ch 3, dc bp around next st, (dc fp around next st, dc bp around next st) across to last st, dc in last st, turn.

Row 3: Ch 3, dc fp around next st, (dc bp around next st, dc fp around next st) across to last st, dc in last st, turn.

Rows 4-6: Repeat rows 2 and 3 alternately, ending with row 2. At end of last row, change to double-ended hook.

Body

Row 1: Ch 1 *(counts as first st)*, pull up lp in each st across leaving all lps on hook, turn. *(35 lps on hook) [37 lps on hook, 39 lps on hook, 43 lps on hook]*

Row 2: With off-white, work lps off hook, **do not turn.**

Row 3: Ch 1, skip first vertical bar, (yo, skip next vertical bar, K in next vertical bar) across, turn.

Row 4: With gray, work lps off hook, **do not turn.**

Row 5: Ch 1, skip first vertical bar; for **inc** *(see Special Stitches)* in next vertical bar, K in next vertical bar, pull up lp in same vertical bar, pull up lp in each vertical bar across to last vertical bar, inc, turn. *(37 lps on hook) [39 lps on hook, 41 lps on hook, 45 lps on hook]*

Rows 6-21 [6-21, 6-25, 6-13]: Repeat rows 2-5 consecutively, ending with *45 [47, 51, 49] lps* on hook in row 20.

Rows 22-24 [22-24, 26-28, 14-16]: Repeat rows 2-4.

Row 25 [25, 29, 17]: Ch 1, skip first vertical bar, pull up lp in each vertical bar across, turn.

Rows 26-28 [26-28, 30-32, 18-20]: Repeat rows 2-4.

Row 29 [29, 33, 21]: Ch 1, skip first vertical bar, inc, pull up lp in each vertical bar across to last vertical bar, inc, turn. *(47 lps on hook) [49 lps on hook, 53 lps on hook, 51 lps on hook]*

Rows 30-93 [30-93, 34-97, 22-109]: Repeat rows 22-29 [22-29, 26-33, 14-21] consecutively, ending with *63 [65, 69, 73] lps* on hook in last row.

Rows 94-108 [94-112, 98-116, 110-120]: Repeat rows 2, 3, 4 and 25 [25, 29, 17] consecutively, ending with row 4.

Row 109 [113, 117, 121]: Ch 1, sl st in each vertical bar across. Fasten off.

Pin center of last row to shoulder seam. Sew last row to Front and Back of Sweater. Sew Sleeve and Side seams.

NECK RIBBING

Rnd 1: Working in ends of rows around neck opening, with I hook and gray, join with sl st in either shoulder seam, ch 3, evenly spacing sts so piece lays flat, dc around, ending with an odd number of sts, join with sl st in top of ch-3.

Rnds 2-4: Ch 3, (dc bp around next st, dc fp around next st) around, join. At end of last rnd, fasten off.♦

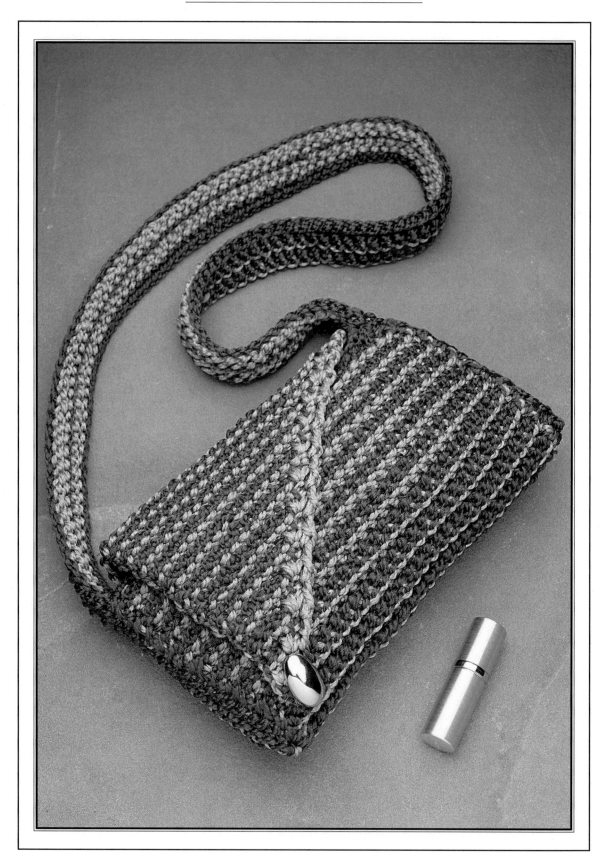

Everyday Essentials Purse

Designed by Sue Penrod

Here's a chic little purse that's the perfect fit for times when you only need to carry the bare necessities!

FINISHED SIZE: 6" x 8" not including Strap.

MATERIALS: Worsted yarn— 2 oz. each dk. blue and lt. blue; 1" decorative shank button; Optional: 9" zipper and zipper pull charm; tapestry needle; J double-ended hook or hook size needed to obtain gauge.

GAUGE: 7 sts = 2"; 8 pattern rows = 1".

NOTES: Read General Instructions on page 6 before beginning pattern.

PURSE

Row 1: With dk. blue, ch 29, pull up lp in second ch from hook and in each ch across leaving all lps on hook, turn. *(29 lps on hook)*

Row 2: With lt. blue, work lps off hook, **do not turn.**

Row 3: Ch 1, skip first vertical bar, pull up lp in each vertical bar across, turn.

Row 4: With dk. blue, work lps off hook, **do not turn.**

Row 5: Ch 1, skip first vertical bar, pull up lp in each vertical bar across, turn.

Row 6: With lt. blue, work lps off hook, **do not turn.**

Rows 7-87: Repeat rows 3-6 consecutively, ending with row 3.

Row 88: For **flap,** with dk. blue, work lps off hook to last 4 lps; for **decrease (dec),** yo, pull through last 4 lps on hook, **do not turn.** *(27)*

Row 89: Ch 1, skip first dec, pull up lp in each vertical bar across, turn.

Row 90: With lt. blue, work lps off hook, **do not turn.**

Row 91: Ch 1, skip first vertical bar, pull up lp in each vertical bar across, turn.

Rows 92-139: Repeat rows 88-91 consecutively, ending with *3 lps on hook* in last row.

Row 140: With dk. blue, pull through one lp on hook, yo, pull through all 3 lps on hook, **turn.** Fasten off dk. blue.

Row 141: With lt. blue, working in ends of rows across slanted edge of flap; for **button loop,** ch 2, skip first dk. blue row; for **edging;** ch 1, working from left to right, **reverse sc** *(see page 160)* in next dk. blue row, (ch 1, reverse sc in next dk. blue row) across slant, sl st in next row. Fasten off.

Strap

Row 1: With dk. blue, ch 150, pull up lp in second ch from hook and in each ch across leaving all lps on hook, turn. *(150 lps on hook)*

Row 2: With lt. blue, work lps off hook, **do not turn.**

Row 3: Ch 1, skip first vertical bar, pull up lp in each vertical bar across, turn.

Row 4: With dk. blue, work lps off hook, **do not turn.**

Row 5: Repeat row 3.

Rows 6-8: Repeat rows 2-4.

Row 9: Ch 1, skip first vertical bar, sl st in each vertical bar across. Fasten off.

Finishing

Fold Purse into thirds so flap will fold down over front of Purse. Sew end of Strap into fold of front and back *(see photo);* repeat with other end of Strap on other side of Purse.

Sew button to front of Purse corresponding to button loop on end of flap.

Optional: With needle and matching thread, sew zipper into Purse opening beneath flap. Attach charm to zipper pull.♦

Multi-Style Winter Hat

DESIGNED BY SUE PENROD

This versatile hat design, worked with a large-size hook for extra softness and one-size convenience, transforms into several fashionable accessories!

FINISHED SIZE: Adult's one size fits all.

MATERIALS: Worsted yarn— 3 oz. each plum and variegated; tapestry needle; K double-ended hook or hook size needed to obtain gauge.

GAUGE: 7 sts = 2"; 10 rows = 1".

NOTES: Read General Instructions on page 6 before beginning pattern.

This design is versatile and may be worn as earmuffs, hat or turtle neck *(see photos)*.

HAT

Row 1: With plum, ch 39, pull up lp in second ch from hook and in each ch across leaving all lps on hook, turn. *(39 lps on hook)*

Row 2: With variegated, work lps off hook, **do not turn.**

Row 3: Ch 1, skip first vertical bar, pull up lp under both strands of each **horizontal bar** *(see illustration)* across, turn.

Horizontal Bar

Row 4: With plum, work lps off hook, **do not turn.**

Row 5: Ch 1, skip first vertical bar, pull up lp under both strand of each horizontal bar across, turn.

Rows 6-196: Repeat rows 2-5 consecutively, ending with row 4.

Row 197: Ch 1, sl st under both strands of each horizontal bar across. Fasten off.

For **seam,** sew 22 sts of first and last rows together.

For **drawstring,** with variegated, ch 75. Fasten off. Weave through every other row on unsewn end of Hat.

For **pompom** (make 2), wrap variegated around two fingers 36 times, slide loops off fingers; tie separate strand around middle of all loops. Cut loops, trim. Sew one to each end of drawstring. Pull up drawstring to close top of Hat, tie into bow. Turn up bottom edge for brim.♦

Crochenit

Snow Puff Scarf

DESIGNED BY CAROLYN CHRISTMAS

Soft as a cloud and rich in texture, this heavenly scarf is a dream to crochet in a luscious combination of baby yarns!

FINISHED SIZE: 74½" long.

MATERIALS: 12 oz. blue baby bulky yarn; 2 oz white pompadour baby yarn; 5" square piece of cardboard; tapestry needle; Crochenit™ hook.

GAUGE: 2 sts = 1".

CROCHENIT™ STITCHES: Basic Stitch #101; High Stitch #104.

SPECIAL STITCH: For **high stitch (high st),** insert hook in next vertical bar, yo, pull lp through, ch 1.

NOTE: Read General Instructions on page 8 before beginning pattern.

SCARF

Row 1: With bulky yarn, ch 150, pull up lp in third ch from hook, ch 1 *(high st made),* **high st** *(see Special Stitch)* in each ch across, turn. *(149 lps on hook)*

Row 2: With baby yarn, work lps off hook, **do not turn.**

Row 3: Skip first vertical bar, pull up lp in each vertical bar across, turn.

Row 4: With bulky yarn, work lps off hook, **do not turn.**

Row 5: Ch 1, skip first vertical bar, high st in each vertical bar across, turn.

Rows 6-56: Repeat rows 2-5 consecutively, ending with row 4.

Row 57: Matching sts, sl st first and last rows together, Fasten off.

Gather and sew opening closed at short ends.

POMPOM (make 2)

With bulky and baby yarns held together, wrap around cardboard completely covering cardboard. Slide loops off cardboard. Tie separate strand of baby yarn tightly around center of all strands. Cut loops. Trim ends.

Sew one Pompom to each end of Scarf.♦

Coat of Many Colors

DESIGNED BY ANN PARNELL

Stitch your odds and ends of worsted yarn into a fashion sensation when you crochet this easy-to-make jacket in a rainbow of colors!

FINISHED SIZE: Instructions given fit 40" bust. Changes for 44", 48" and 52" bust sizes are in [ ].

MATERIALS: Worsted yarn—18 [20, 23, 26] oz. each gray and assorted scrap colors; eight ¾" buttons; 4 stitch markers or bobby pins; tapestry needle; N double-ended and I hooks or hook sizes needed to obtain gauges.

GAUGES: With **N double-ended hook,** 3 sts = 1"; 11 pattern rows = 2". With **I hook,** 7 sc = 2"; 4 sc rows worked in **back lps** *(see page 160)* = 1".

NOTES: Read General Instructions on page 6 before beginning pattern.

Use double-ended hook unless otherwise stated.

BACK

Row 1: With gray, ch 54 [60, 66, 72], pull up lp in second ch from hook, pull up lp in each ch across leaving all lps on hook, turn. *(54 lps on hook)* [60 lps on hook, 66 lps on hook, 72 lps on hook]

Row 2: With any scrap color, work lps off hook, **do not turn.**

Row 3: Ch 1, skip first vertical bar, pull up lp in each vertical bar across, turn.

Row 4: With gray, work lps off hook, **do not turn.**

Row 5: Ch 1, skip first vertical bar, pull up lp in each vertical bar across, turn.

Row 6: With next scrap color, work lps off hook, **do not turn.**

Rows 7-106: Repeat rows 3-6 consecutively.

Rows 107: For **armhole shaping,** sl st in first 5 [7, 8, 9] vertical bars, ch 1, pull up lp in each vertical bar across, turn. *(50 lps on hook)* [54 lps on hook, 59 lps on hook, 64 lps on hook]

Row 108: With gray, work lps off hook, **do not turn.**

Row 109: Repeat row 107. *(46 lps on hook)* [48 lps on hook, 52 lps on hook, 56 lps on hook]

Row 110: With next scrap color, work lps off hook, **do not turn.**

Rows 111-156 [111-160, 111-164, 111-168]: Repeat rows 3-6 consecutively, ending with row 4.

Row 157 [161, 165, 169]: Ch 1, skip first vertical bar, sl st in each vertical bar across. Fasten off.

FIRST FRONT

Row 1: With gray, ch 28, [31, 34, 38], pull up lp in second ch from hook and in each ch across leaving all lps on hook, turn. *(28 lps on hook) [31 lps on hook, 34 lps on hook, 38 lps on hook]*

Row 2: With scrap color, work lps off hook, **do not turn.**

Rows 3-108: Repeat rows 3-6 of Back consecutively, ending with row 4.

Row 109: Repeat row 107 of Back. *(24 lps on hook) [25 lps on hook, 27 lps on hook, 30 lps on hook]*

Row 110: With next scrap color, work lps off hook across to last 3 lps on hook; for **neck shaping,** yo, pull through last 3 lps, **do not turn.**

Row 111: Ch 1, skip first vertical bar, pull up lp in each vertical bar across, turn. *(23 lps on hook) [24 lps on hook, 26 lps on hook, 29 lps on hook]*

Row 112: With gray, work lps off hook, **do not turn.**

Row 113: Ch 1, skip first vertical bar, pull up lp in each vertical bar across, turn.

Rows 114-160: Repeat rows 110-113 rows consecutively, ending with row 112 and *11 [12, 14, 17] lps on hook* in last row.

Rows 161-162: Repeat rows 5 and 6 of Back.

Rows 163-164 [163-164, 163-168, 163-168]: Repeat rows 3 and 4 of Back [3 and 4 of Back, 3-6 of Back consecutively, 3-6 of Back consecutively], ending with row 4.

Row 165 [165, 169, 169]: Ch 1, skip first vertical bar, sl st in each vertical bar across. Fasten off.

SECOND FRONT

Row 1: With gray, ch 28, [31, 34, 38], pull up lp in second ch from hook and in each ch across leaving all lps on hook, turn. *(28 lps on hook) [31 lps on hook, 34 lps on hook, 38 lps on hook]*

Row 2: With scrap color, work lps off hook, **do not turn.**

Rows 3-106: Repeat rows 3-6 of Back consecutively.

Row 107: Repeat same row of Back. *(24 lps on hook) [25 lps on hook, 27 lps on hook, 30 lps on hook]*

Rows 108-109: Repeat rows 4 and 5 of Back.

Row 110: With next scrap color; for **neck shaping,** yo, pull through first 2 lps on hook; (yo, pull through 2 lps on hook) across, **do not turn.**

Row 111: Ch 1, skip first vertical bar, pull up lp in each vertical bar across, turn. *(23 lps on hook) [24 lps on hook, 26 lps on hook, 29 lps on hook]*

Row 112: With gray, work lps off hook, **do not turn.**

Row 113: Ch 1, skip first vertical bar, pull up lp in each vertical bar across, turn.

Rows 114-160: Repeat rows 110-113 consecutively, ending with row 112 and *11 [12, 14, 17] lps on hook* in last row.

Rows 161-162: Repeat rows 5 and 6 of Back.

Rows 163-164 [163-164, 163-168, 163-168]: Repeat rows 3 and 4 of Back [3 and 4 of Back, 3-6 of Back consecutively, 3-6 of Back consecutively], ending with row 4.

Row 165 [165, 169, 169]: Ch 1, skip first vertical bar, sl st in each vertical bar across. Fasten off.

SLEEVE (make 2)

Row 1: With gray, ch 14 [16, 20, 24], pull up lp in second ch from hook, pull up lp in each ch across leaving all lps on hook, turn. *(14 lps on hook) [16 lps on hook, 20 lps on hook, 24 lps on hook]*

Row 2: With any scrap color, work lps off hook, **do not turn.**

Row 3: Ch 1, skip first vertical bar, pull up lp in each vertical bar across, turn.

Row 4: With gray, work lps off hook, **do not turn.**

Row 5: Ch 1, skip first vertical bar, pull up lp in each vertical bar across, turn.

Rows 6: With next scrap color, work lps off hook, **do not turn.**

Row 7: Ch 1, skip first vertical bar, pull up lp in each vertical bar across, turn.

Row 8: With gray, work lps off hook, **do not turn.**

Row 9: Ch 1, skip first vertical bar, pull up lp in top strand of next **horizontal bar** *(see illustration)*, pull up lp in each vertical bar across to last vertical bar, pull up lp in top strand of next horizontal bar, pull up lp in last vertical bar, turn. *(16 lps on hook) [18 lps on hook, 22 lps on hook, 26 lps on hook]*

Horizontal Bar

Rows 10-136: Repeat rows 2-9 consecutively, ending with row 8 and *46 [48, 52, 56] lps on hook.*

Row 137: Ch 1, skip first vertical bar, sl st in each vertical bar across. Fasten off.

Sew shoulder seams. Easing to fit, sew Sleeves into armholes *(refer to diagram).*

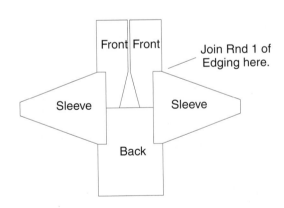

EDGING

Rnd 1: With I hook, working in ends of rows and in sts around outer edge of Sweater, evenly spacing sts so piece lays flat, join gray with sc in seam near armhole as shown in diagram, sc around entire Sweater with 3 sc in each corner of Fronts and back and 2 sc in row at beginning of neck shaping on each Front, join with sl st in first sc, **turn.**

*Note: Work remaining rnds in **back lps** only.*

Rnd 2: Ch 1, sc in each st around with 3 sc in each center corner s and 2 sc in first st of each 2-sc increase on Front, join, **turn.**

Rnds 3-4: Ch 1, sc in each st around with 3 sc in each center corner st, join, **turn.**

Note: With bobby pins or stitch markers, mark first st at beginning of neck shaping on right Front; working down toward bottom of Sweater, (skip next 11 sts, place marker in next st) 3 times.

Rnd 5: Ch 1, work in established sc pattern across to bottom corner of right Front with 3 sc in corner st; for **buttonholes,** (sc in each st across to next marked st, ch 1, skip next marked st) 4 times, work in established sc pattern around, join, **turn.**

Rnd 6: Ch 1, sc in each st and in each ch around with 3 sc in each center corner st, join, **turn.**

Rnds 7-8: Work in established pattern around, join, **turn.** At end of last rnd, fasten off.

Sew underarm and side seams on each side leaving 7" unsewn at bottom for slits. For **cuffs,** turn Edging up at bottom of each Sleeve.

Sew four buttons to Edging opposite buttonholes. Sew remaining buttons to other side of Edging opposite buttonholes. *(Sweater is reversible.)*♦

Pebbles Duster

DESIGNED BY MARGRET WILLSON

Eye-catching color and bold, scalloped stripes create the stand-out design in this stunning, coat-style cardigan that's the perfect accent to dress up casual attire or compliment a stylish outfit.

FINISHED SIZE: Instructions given fit women's 40" bust (medium), changes for 45" bust (large) and 50" bust (X-large) are in [ ].

MATERIALS: Worsted yarn—18 [20, 24] oz. each of lavender and green, 16 [18, 22] oz. of black; 8 shank ¾" buttons; sewing thread, sewing and tapestry needles; I crochet hook and K double-ended swivel hook or hook size needed to obtain gauge.

GAUGE: With **double-ended hook,** 14 sts = 4"; 14 pattern rows = 3".

SPECIAL STITCHES: For **knit stitch (K,** *see illustration),* insert hook between front and back vertical bars and under horizontal bar of next st, yo, pull lp through.

Knit stitch

For **dc lp,** yo, insert hook between front and back vertical bars and under horizontal bar of next st, yo, pull lp through, yo, pull through 2 lps on hook.

For **tr lp,** yo 2 times, insert hook between front and back vertical bars and under horizontal bar of next st, yo, pull lp through, (yo, pull through 2 lps on hook) 2 times.

For **decrease (dec),** insert hook in next 2 vertical bars at same time, yo, pull lp through.

NOTES: Read General Instructions on page 6 before beginning pattern.

Use double-ended hook unless otherwise stated.

DUSTER

Row 1: With black, ch 147 [163, 179], pull up lp in second ch from hook, pull up lp in each ch across, turn. *(147 lps on hook) [163 lps on hook,*

179 lps on hook]

Row 2: With green, work lps off hook, **do not turn.**

Row 3: Ch 1, skip first vertical bar, **K** *(see Special Stitches),* ***dc lp** *(see Special Stitches),* **tr lp** *(see Special Stitches),* dc lp, K; repeat from * across to last vertical bar, pull up lp in last vertical bar, turn.

Row 4: With black, work lps off hook, **do not turn.**

Row 5: Ch 1, skip first vertical bar, pull up lp in each vertical bar across, turn.

Row 6: With lavender, work lps off hook, **do not turn.**

Row 7: Ch 1, skip first vertical bar, K, (dc lp, tr lp, dc lp, K) across to last vertical bar, pull up lp in last vertical bar, turn.

Row 8: With black, work lps off hook, **do not turn.**

Row 9: Ch 1, skip first vertical bar, pull up lp in each vertical bar across, turn.

Rows 10-116: Repeat rows 2-9 consecutively, ending with row 4.

Row 117: For **first front,** ch 1, skip first vertical bar, pull up lp in each of next 26 [30, 34] vertical bars leaving remaining bars unworked, turn. *(27 lps on hook), [31 lps on hook, 35 lps on hook]*

Rows 118-121: Repeat rows 6-9.

Row 122-148 [122-148, 122-156]: Repeat rows 2-9 consecutively, ending with row 4.

Row 149 [149, 157]: For **shoulder,** with black, skip first vertical bar, sl st in next 6 vertical bars, pull up lp in each vertical bar across, turn. *(21 lps on hook) [25 lps on hook, 29 lps on hook]*

Row 150 [150, 158]: With lavender, work lps off hook, **do not turn.**

Row 151 [151, 159]: Ch 1, skip first vertical bar, K, (dc lp, tr lp, dc lp, K) across to last 3 vertical bars, dc lp, tr lp, dc lp, turn.

Row 152 [152, 160]: With black, work lps off hook, **do not turn.**

Row 153 [153, 161]: Ch 1, skip first vertical bar, **dec** *(see Special Stitches),* pull up lp in each vertical bar across, turn. *(20 lps on hook) [24 lps on hook, 28 lps on hook]*

Row 154 [154, 162]: With green, work lps off hook, **do not turn.**

Row 155 [155, 163]: Ch 1, skip first vertical bar, K, (dc lp, tr lp, dc lp, K) across to last 2 vertical bars, dc lp, tr lp, turn.

Row 156 [156, 164]: With black, work lps off hook, **do not turn.**

Row 157 [157, 165]: Ch 1, skip first vertical bar, dec, pull up lp in each vertical bar across, turn. *(19 lps on hook) [23 lps on hook, 27 lps on hook]*

Row 158 [158, 166]: With lavender, work lps off hook, **do not turn.**

Row 159 [159, 167]: Ch 1, skip first vertical bar, K, (dc lp, tr lp, dc lp, K) across to last vertical bar, pull up lp in last vertical bar, turn.

Rows 160-161 [160-161, 168-169]: Repeat rows 152-153 [152-153, 160-161]. *(18 lps on hook) [22 lps on hook, 26 lps on hook]*

Row 162 [162, 170]: With green, work lps off hook, **do not turn.**

Row 163 [163, 171]: Ch 1, skip first vertical bar, K, (dc lp, tr lp, dc lp, K) across to last 4 vertical bars, dc lp, tr lp, dc lp, pull up lp in last vertical bar, turn.

Row 164 [164, 172]: With black, work lps off hook, **do not turn.**

Row 165 [165, 173]: Ch 1, sl st in each vertical bar across. Fasten off.

Row 117: With predominately green and lavender side facing you, join black with sl st in first unworked vertical bar on row 116, sl st in next 15 [17, 17] vertical bars *(armhole made),* for **back,** pull up lp in each of next 62 [66, 74] vertical bars leaving remaining vertical bars unworked, turn. *(63 lps on hook) [67 lps on hook, 75 lps on hook]*

Rows 118-121: Repeat rows 6-9.

Rows 122-164 [122-164, 122-172]: Repeat rows 2-9 consecutively, ending with row 4.

Row 165 [165, 173]: Ch 1, sl st in each vertical bar across. Fasten off

Row 117: With predominately green and lavender side facing, join black with sl st in first unworked vertical bar on row 116, sl st in next 15 [17, 17] vertical bars *(armhole made),* for **front,**

pull up lp in each of last 26 [30, 34] vertical bars, turn. *(27 lps on hook) [31 lps on hook, 35 lps on hook]*

Rows 118-121: Repeat rows 6-9.

Row 122-148 [133-148, 122-156]: Repeat rows 2-9 consecutively, ending with row 4.

Row 149 [149, 157]: For **shoulder,** ch 1, skip first vertical bar, pull up lp in each of next 20 [24, 28] vertical bars leaving last 6 vertical bars unworked, turn. *(21 lps on hook), [25 lps on hook, 29 lps on hook]*

Row 150 [150, 158]: With lavender, work lps off hook, **do not turn.**

Row 151 [151, 159]: Ch 1, skip first vertical bar, K, (dc lp, tr lp, dc lp, K) across to last 3 vertical bars, dc lp, tr lp, dc lp, turn.

Row 152 [152, 160]: With black, work lps off hook, **do not turn.**

Row 153 [153, 161]: Ch 1, skip first vertical bar, pull up lp in each vertical bar across to last 3 vertical bars, dec, pull up lp in last vertical bar, turn. *(20 lps on hook) [24 lps on hook, 28 lps on hook]*

Row 154 [154, 162]: With green, work lps off hook, **do not turn.**

Row 155 [155, 163]: Ch 1, skip first vertical bar, K, (dc lp, tr lp, dc lp, K) across to last 2 vertical bars, dc lp, tr lp, turn.

Row 156 [156, 164]: With black, work lps off hook, **do not turn.**

Row 157 [157, 165]: Ch 1, skip first vertical bar, pull up lp in each vertical bar across to last 3 vertical bars, dec, pull up lp in last vertical bar, turn. *(19 lps on hook) [23 lps on hook, 27 lps on hook]*

Row 158 [158, 166]: With lavender, work lps off hook, **do not turn.**

Row 159 [159, 167]: Ch 1, skip first vertical bar, K, (dc lp, tr lp, dc lp, K) across to last vertical bar, pull up lp in last vertical bar, turn.

Rows 160-161 [160-161, 168-169]: Repeat rows 152-153 [152-153, 160-161]. *(18 lps on hook) [22 lps on hook, 26 lps on hook]*

Row 162 [162, 170]: With green, work lps off hook, **do not turn.**

Row 163 [163, 171]: Ch 1, skip first vertical bar, K, (dc lp, tr lp, dc lp, K) across to last 4 vertical bars, dc lp, tr lp, dc lp, pull up lp in last vertical bar, turn.

Row 164 [164, 172]: With black, work lps off hook, **do not turn.**

Row 165 [165, 173]: Ch 1, sl st in each vertical bar across. Fasten off.

Sew shoulder seams together.

SLEEVE (make 2)

Row 1: With black, ch 35, [39, 43], pull up lp in second ch from hook, pull up lp in each ch across, turn. *(35 lps on hook) [39 lps on hook, 43 lps on hook]*

Rows 2-16: Repeat rows 2-9 of Duster consecutively, ending with row 8.

Row 17: Ch 1, pull up lp in first vertical bar *(increase made)*, pull up lp in each vertical bar across to last **horizontal bar** *(see illustration)*, pull up lp in top strand of last horizontal bar *(increase made)*, pull up lp in last vertical bar, turn. *(37 lps on hook) [41 lps on hook, 45 lps on hook]*

Horizontal Bar

Row 18: With green, work lps off hook, **do not turn.**

Row 19: Ch 1, skip first vertical bar, K, (dc lp, tr lp, dc lp, K) across to last 3 vertical bars, dc lp, tr lp, pull up lp in last vertical bar, turn.

Row 20: With black, work lps off hook, **do not turn.**

Row 21: Repeat row 17. *(39 lps on hook) [43 lps on hook, 47 lps on hook]*

Row 22: With lavender, work lps off hook, **do not turn.**

Row 23: Ch 1, skip first vertical bar, K, (dc lp, tr lp, dc lp, K) across to last vertical bar, pull up lp in last vertical bar, turn.

Row 24: With black, work lps off hook, **do not turn.**

Row 25: Repeat row 17. *(41 lps on hook) [45 lps on hook, 49 lps on hook]*

Row 26: With green, work lps off hook, **do not turn.**

Row 27: Ch 1, skip first vertical bar, K, (dc lp, tr lp, dc lp, K) across to last 3 sts, dc lp, tr lp, pull up lp in last vertical bar, turn.

Row 28: With black, work lps off hook, **do not turn.**

Row 29: Repeat row 17. *(43 lps on hook) [47 lps on hook, 51 lps on hook]*

Row 30: With lavender, work lps off hook, **do not turn.**

Row 31: Ch 1, skip first vertical bar, K, (dc lp, tr lp, dc lp, K) across to last vertical bar, pull up lp in last vertical bar, turn.

Row 32: With black, work lps off hook, **do not turn.**

Row 33: Repeat row 17. *(45 lps on hook) [49 lps on hook, 53 lps on hook]*

Row 34: With green, work lps off hook, **do not turn.**

Row 35: Ch 1, skip first vertical bar, K, (dc lp, tr lp, dc lp, K) across to last 3 vertical bars, dc lp, tr lp, pull up lp in last vertical bar, turn.

Row 36: With black, work lps off hook, **do not turn.**

Row 37: Repeat row 17. *(47 lps on hook) [51 lps on hook, 55 lps on hook]*

Row 38: With lavender, work lps off hook, **do not turn.**

Row 39: Ch 1, skip first vertical bar, K, (dc lp, tr lp, dc lp, K) across to last vertical bar, pull up lp in last vertical bar, turn.

Row 40: With black, work lps off hook, **do not turn.**

Row 41: Repeat row 17. *(49 lps on hook) [53 lps on hook, 57 lps on hook]*

Row 42: With green, work lps off hook, **do not turn.**

Row 43: Ch 1, skip first vertical bar, K, (dc lp, tr lp, dc lp, K) across to last 3 vertical bars, dc lp, tr lp, pull up lp in last vertical bar, turn.

Row 44: With black, work lps off hook, **do not turn.**

Row 45: Repeat row 17. *(51 lps on hook) [55 lps on hook, 59 lps on hook]*

Row 46: With lavender, work lps off hook, **do not turn.**

Row 47: Ch 1, skip first vertical bar, K, (dc lp, tr lp, dc lp, K) across to last vertical bar, pull up lp in last vertical bar, turn.

Row 48: With black, work lps off hook, **do not turn.**

Row 49: Repeat row 17. *(53 lps on hook) [57 lps on hook, 61 lps on hook]*

continued on page 52

Coffee Cardigan

Coffee Cardigan

Designed by Margret Willson

The easy style and rich, café au lait colors of this delicious design create a fun-and-fashionable cardigan that's made in only three pieces!

FINISHED SIZES: Lady's chest 36"-38" (medium). Finished measurement 40". Lady's chest 40"-42" (large). Finished measurement 45". Lady's chest, 44"-46" (X-large). Finished measurement 50".

Instructions are for medium; changes for large and X-large are in [ ].

MATERIALS: Worsted yarn—19 [20, 22] oz. lt. brown, 15 [16, 18] oz. brown; 2 shank ⅝" buttons; brown sewing thread; sewing and tapestry needles; H crochet and J double-ended hooks or hook size needed to obtain gauge.

GAUGE: With **double-ended hook,** 19 sts = 5"; 10 rows = 3".

SPECIAL STITCH: For **dc loop (dc lp),** yo, insert hook in top of next shell, pull lp through, yo, pull through 2 lps on hook.

NOTES: Read General Instructions on page 6 before beginning pattern.

Use double-ended hook unless otherwise stated.

CARDIGAN

Row 1: Starting at bottom, with brown, ch 152 [170, 188], pull up lp in second ch from hook, pull up lp in each ch across, turn. *(152 lps on hook) [170 lps on hook, 188 lps on hook]*

Row 2: With lt. brown, pull through one lp on hook, *ch 1, yo, pull through 3 lps on hook *(shell completed);* repeat from * across to last 2 lps on hook, yo, pull through last 2 lps on hook, **do not turn.**

Row 3: Ch 1, skip first vertical bar, 2 **dc lp** *(see Special Stitch)* in top of each shell across to last vertical bar, dc lp in last vertical bar, turn.

Row 4: With brown, work lps off hook, **do not turn.**

Row 5: Ch 1, skip first vertical bar, pull up lp in each vertical bar across, turn.

Rows 6-64: Repeat rows 2-5 consecutively, ending with row 4.

Row 65: For **first front,** ch 1, skip first vertical bar, pull up lp in each of next 35 [41, 45] vertical bars leaving remaining bars unworked, turn. *(36 lps on hook) [42 lps on hook, 46 lps on hook]*

Rows 66-88 [66-92, 66-96]: Repeat rows 2-5 consecutively, ending with row 4.

Row 89 [93, 97]: For **shoulder,** skip first vertical bar, sl st in next 12 [14, 14] vertical bars, pull up lp in each vertical bar across, turn. *(24 lps on hook) [28 lps on hook, 32 lps on hook]*

Rows 90-100 [94-104, 98-108]: Repeat rows 2-5 consecutively, ending with row 4.

Row 101 [105, 109]: Ch 1, sl st in each vertical bar across. Fasten off.

Row 65: For **back,** with brown, pull up lp in next 80 [86, 96] vertical bars on row 64, leaving remaining lps unworked, turn.

Rows 66-100 [66-104, 66-108]: Repeat rows 2-5 consecutively, ending with row 4.

Row 101 [105, 109]: Ch 1, sl st in each vertical bar across. Fasten off.

Row 65: For **second front,** with brown, pull up lp in last 36 [42, 46] vertical bars, turn.

Rows 66-88 [66-92, 66-96]: Repeat rows 2-5 consecutively, ending with row 4.

Row 89 [93, 97]: For **shoulder,** ch 1, skip first vertical bar, pull up lp in next 24 [28, 32] vertical bars leaving last 12 [14, 14] bars unworked, turn.

Rows 90-100 [94-104, 98-108]: Repeat rows 2-5 consecutively, ending with row 4.

Row 101 [105, 109]: Ch 1, sl st in each st across. Fasten off.

Matching sts, sew shoulder seams on fronts and back together.

Sleeve (make 2)

Row 1: Starting at bottom, with brown, ch 66 [74, 82], pull up lp in second ch from hook, pull up lp in each ch across, turn. *(66 lps on hook) [74 lps on hook, 82 lps on hook]*

Row 2: With lt. brown, pull through one lp on hook, *ch 1, yo, pull through 3 lps on hook *(shell completed);* repeat from * across to last 2 lps on hook, yo, pull through last 2 lps on hook, **do not turn.**

Row 3: Ch 1, skip first vertical bar, 2 dc lp in top of each shell across to last vertical bar, dc lp in last vertical bar, turn.

Row 4: With brown, work lps off hook, **do not turn.**

Row 5: Ch 1, skip first vertical bar, pull up lp in each vertical bar across, turn.

Rows 6-64: Repeat rows 2-5 consecutively, ending with row 4.

Row 65: Ch 1, sl st in each vertical bar across. Fasten off.

For **armhole trim,** working around outer edge of one armhole, with H hook and brown, join with sc in any st at underarm, evenly space 65 [73, 81] more sc around outer edge, join with sl st in first sc. Fasten off. Repeat armhole trim on other armhole.

Matching last row on Sleeves to armhole trim, sew Sleeves to armholes. Sew Sleeve seams.

Cuff

Rnd 1: Working in starting ch on opposite side of row 1 on one Sleeve, with H hook and brown, join with sl st in first st, ch 1, sc first 2 sts tog, (sc next 2 sts tog) around, join with sl st in first sc. *(33 sc made) [37 sc made, 41 sc made]*

Rnds 2-7: Ch 1, sc in each st around, join. At end of last rnd, fasten off.
Repeat on other Sleeve.

Trim

Rnd 1: Working around outer edge of Cardigan, in sts, in ends of rows and in starting ch on opposite side of row 1, with H hook and brown, join with sc in st at back of neck, evenly spacing sts so piece lays flat, sc around with sc 3 sts tog at shoulder shaping indentation and 3 sc in each corner, join with sl st in first sc.

Rnd 2: Ch 1, sc in each st around to one st before first 3 sc dec, sc next 3 sts tog, (sc in each st around to center st next 3-sc group, 3 sc in center st) 4 times, sc in each st around to one st before next 3 sc dec, sc next 3 sts tog, sc in each st around, join.

Rnd 3: Ch 1, sc in each st around to one st before next 3 sc dec, sc next 3 sts tog, (sc in each st around to center st of next 3 sc group, 3 sc in center st) 3 times, sc in each st around to 8 sts before center st of next 3-sc group, ch 2, skip next 2 sts, sc in next 4 sts, ch 2, skip next 2 sts *(buttonholes made),* 3 sc in next center corner st, sc in each st around to one st before next 3-sc dec, sc next 3 sts tog, sc in each st around, join.

Rnd 4: Ch 1, sc in each st and in each ch around with 3 sc in each center corner st, join.

Rnd 5: Ch 1, sc in each st around with 3-sc in each center corner st, join. Fasten off.
Sew buttons to front opposite buttonholes.♦

Pebbles Duster
continued from page 49

continued from page 49

Row 50: With green, work lps off hook, **do not turn.**

Row 51: Ch 1, skip first vertical bar, K, (dc lp, tr lp, dc lp, K) across to last 3 vertical bars, dc lp, tr lp, pull up lp in last vertical bar, turn.

Row 52: With black, work lps off hook, **do not turn.**

Row 53: Repeat row 17. *(55 lps on hook) [59 lps on hook, 63 lps on hook]*

Row 54: With lavender, work lps off hook, **do not turn.**

Row 55: Ch 1, skip first vertical bar, K, (dc lp, tr lp, dc lp, K) across to last vertical bar, pull up lp in last vertical bar, turn.

Row 56: With black, work lps off hook, **do not turn.**

Row 57: Repeat row 17. *(57 lps on hook) [61 lps on hook, 65 lps on hook]*

Row 58: With green, work lps off hook, **do not turn.**

Row 59: Ch 1, skip first vertical bar, K, (dc lp, tr lp, dc lp, K) across to last 3 vertical bars, dc lp, tr lp, pull up lp in last vertical bar, turn.

Row 60: With black, work lps off hook, **do**

not turn.

Row 61: Repeat row 17. *(59 lps on hook) [63 lps on hook, 67 lps on hook]*

Row 62: With lavender, work lps off hook, **do not turn.**

Row 63: Ch 1, skip first vertical bar, K, (dc lp, tr lp, dc lp, K) across to last vertical bar, pull up lp in last vertical bar, turn.

Row 64: With black, work lps off hook, **do not turn.**

Row 65: Repeat row 17. *(61 lps on hook) [65 lps on hook, 69 lps on hook]*

Row 66: With green, work lps off hook, **do not turn.**

Row 67: Ch 1, skip first vertical bar, K, (dc lp, tr lp, dc lp, K) across to last 3 vertical bars, dc lp, tr lp, pull up lp in last vertical bar, turn.

Row 68: With black, work lps off hook, **do not turn.**

Row 69: Repeat row 17. *(63 lps on hook) [67 lps on hook, 71 lps on hook]*

Row 70: With lavender, work lps off hook, **do not turn.**

Row 71: Ch 1, skip first vertical bar, K, (dc lp, tr lp, dc lp, K) across to last vertical bar, pull up lp in last vertical bar, turn.

Row 72: With black, work lps off hook, **do not turn.**

Row 73: Repeat row 17. *(65 lps on hook) [69 lps on hook, 73 lps on hook]*

Row 74: With green, work lps off hook, **do not turn.**

Row 75: Ch 1, skip first vertical bar, K, (dc lp, tr lp, dc lp, K) across to last 3 vertical bars, dc lp, tr lp, pull up lp in last vertical bar, turn.

Row 76: With black, work lps off hook, **do not turn.**

Row 77: Repeat row 17. *(67 lps on hook) [71 lps on hook, 75 lps on hook]*

Row 78: With lavender, work lps off hook, **do not turn.**

Row 79: Ch 1, skip first vertical bar, K, (dc lp, tr lp, dc lp, K) across to last vertical bar, pull up lp in last vertical bar, turn.

Row 80: With black, work lps off hook, **do not turn.**

Row 81: Repeat row 17. *(69 lps on hook) [73 lps on hook, 77 lps on hook]*

Row 82: With green, work lps off hook, **do not turn.**

Row 83: Ch 1, skip first vertical bar, K, (dc lp, tr lp, dc lp, K) across to last 3 vertical bars, dc lp, tr lp, pull up lp in last vertical bar, turn.

Row 84: With black, work lps off hook, **do not turn.**

Row 85: Repeat row 17. *(71 lps on hook) [75 lps on hook, 79 lps on hook]*

Row 86: With lavender, work lps off hook, **do not turn.**

Row 87: Ch 1, skip first vertical bar, K, (dc lp, tr lp, dc lp, K) across to last vertical bar, pull up lp in last vertical bar, turn

Row 88: With black, work lps off hook, **do not turn.**

Row 89: Ch 1, sl st in each vertical bar across. Fasten off.

Easing to fit, sew last row of Sleeves to armhole. Sew Sleeve seams.

PLACKET

Row 1: With predominantly green and lavender side facing you, working in ends of rows and in sts around outer edge, with I hook and black, join with sc in row 1 on right front, evenly space 107 [110, 113] more sc across to row 149 [149, 157] at shoulder, 3 sc in end of next row, evenly space sc around neckline to row 149 [149, 157] on other side, 3 sc in end of next row, evenly space 108 [111, 114] across ending in end of row 1 on left Front, turn.

Row 2: Ch 1, sc in each st across with 3 sc in center st of each 3-sc group, turn.

Row 3: For **buttonholes,** ch 1, sc in first 8 [4, 7] sts, ch 2, skip next 2 sts, *sc in next 12 [13, 13] sts, ch 2, skip next 2 sts; repeat from * 6 more times, sc in each st across to center st of next 3-sc group, 3 sc in center st, sc in each st across to center st of next 3-sc group, 3 sc in center st, sc in each st across, turn.

Row 4: Ch 1, sc in each st and in each ch across with 3 sc in center st of each 3-sc group, turn.

Row 5: Ch 1, sc in each st across with 3 sc in center st of each 3-sc group. Fasten off.

Sew buttons to Placket opposite buttonholes.♦

Chapter Two

Cherished Children

Heart Puffs

DESIGNED BY MARY ANN SIPES

Pretty panels of soft, puffy hearts will wrap your little sweetheart in loving warmth with an adorable blanket that's almost as precious as she is!

SIZE: 31" x 43".

MATERIALS: Pompadour sport yarn—10 oz. each pink and white; G double-ended and F hooks or hook size needed to obtain gauge.

GAUGE: With **double-ended hook,** 5 sts = 1"; 8 rows = 1".

SPECIAL STITCH: For **puff stitch (puff st),** yo, draw up lp in next vertical bar of same-color row 4 rows below, (yo, draw up lp in same vertical bar) 2 times, yo, draw through 6 lps on hook, ch 1. Skip next horizontal bar on last row.

NOTES: Read General Instructions on page 6 before beginning pattern.

Use double-ended hook unless otherwise stated.

PANEL (make 4)

Row 1: With pink, ch 31, draw up lp in second ch from hook, draw up lp in each ch across, turn. *(31 lps on hook)*

Row 2: With white, work lps off hook, **do not turn.**

Row 3: Ch 1, skip first vertical bar, draw up lp in top strand of each **horizontal bar** across *(see illustration),* turn.

Horizontal Bar

Row 4: With pink, work lps off hook, **do not turn.**

Row 5: Ch 1, skip first vertical bar, draw up lp in top strand of next 5 horizontal bars, **puff st** *(see Special Stitch),* draw up lp in top strand of next 18 horizontal bars, puff st, draw up lp in top strand of last 5 horizontal bars, turn.

Row 6: With white, work lps off hook, **do not turn.**

Row 7: Repeat row 5.

Row 8: With pink, work lps off hook, **do not turn.**

Row 9: Ch 1, skip first vertical bar, (draw up lp in top strand of next 3 horizontal bars, puff st) 2 times, draw up lp in next 14 horizontal bars, (puff st, draw up lp in top strand of next 3 horizontal bars) 2 times, turn.

Row 10: With white, work lps off hook, **do not turn.**

Row 11: Repeat row 9.

Row 12: With pink, work lps off hook, **do not turn.**

Rows 13-15: Repeat rows 5-7.

Row 16: With pink, work lps off hook, **do not turn.**

Row 17: Ch 1, skip first vertical bar, draw up lp in top strand of each horizontal bar across, turn.

Row 18: With white, work lps off hook, **do not turn.**

Row 19: Ch 1, skip first vertical bar, draw up lp in top strand of each horizontal bar across, turn.

Rows 20-24: Repeat rows 16-19 consecutively, ending with row 16.

Row 25: Ch 1, skip first vertical bar, draw up lp in top strand of next 14 horizontal bars, puff st, draw up lp in last 15 horizontal bars, turn.

Row 26: With white, work lps off hook, **do not turn.**

Row 27: Repeat row 25.

Row 28: With pink, work lps off hook, **do not turn.**

Row 29: Ch 1, skip first vertical bar, draw up lp in top strand of next 12 horizontal bars, puff st, draw up lp in top strand of next 3 horizontal bars, puff st, draw up lp in top strand of last 13 horizontal bars, turn.

Row 30: With white, work lps off hook, **do not turn.**

Row 31: Repeat row 29.

Row 32: With pink, work lps off hook, **do not turn.**

Row 33: Ch 1, skip first vertical bar, draw up lp in top strand of next 10 horizontal bars, puff st,

continued on page 61

Teddy Bear

<small>DESIGNED BY SUE PENROD</small>

Stitched in a delightful combination of worsted and bulky yarns, this cuddly little fellow is ready to share a hug and listen to whispered secrets!

SIZE: 18" tall.

MATERIALS: Worsted yarn—5 oz. tan and small amount black; 5 oz. cream bulky yarn; 20" desired color ⅜" grosgrain ribbon; polyester fiberfill; tapestry needle; J double-ended and J hooks or hook size needed to obtain gauge.

GAUGE: With **double-ended hook,** 4 sts = 1"; 6 rows = 1".

NOTES: Read General Instructions on page 6 before beginning pattern.

Use double-ended hook unless otherwise stated.

HEAD & BODY

Row 1: Starting at bottom of Body, with tan, ch 40, draw up lp in second ch from hook, draw up lp in each ch across, turn. *(40 lps on hook)*

Row 2: With cream, work lps off hook, **do not turn.**

Row 3: Ch 1, skip first vertical bar, draw up lp in each vertical bar across, turn.

Row 4: With tan, work lps off hook, **do not turn.**

Row 5: Ch 1, skip first vertical bar, draw up lp in each vertical bar across, turn.

Rows 6-48: Repeat rows 2-5 consecutively, ending with row 4.

Row 49: For **neck shaping,** ch 1, insert hook in first 3 vertical bars at same time, yo, draw lp through, (insert hook in next 2 vertical bars at same time, yo, draw lp through) across to last 3 vertical bars, insert hook in last 3 vertical bars at same time, yo, draw lp through, turn. *(20 lps on hook)*

Row 50: With cream, work lps off hook, **do not turn.**

Row 51: Ch 1, skip first vertical bar, draw up lp in each of next 4 vertical bars, draw up lp in top strand of next **horizontal bar** *(see illustration),* (draw up lp in next vertical bar, draw up lp in top strand of next horizontal bar) 9 times, draw up lp in each of last 6 vertical bars, turn. *(30 lps on hook)*

Horizontal Bar

Rows 52-53: Repeat rows 4 and 5.

Rows 54-76: Repeat rows 2-5 consecutively, ending with row 4.

Row 77: For **head shaping,** repeat row 49. *(15 lps on hook)*

Rows 78-79: Repeat rows 2 and 3. At end of last row, **do not turn,** yo, draw through all lps on hook to gather top of Head, ch 1. Leaving long end for sewing, fasten off.

Weave a separate strand of cream through sts of row 49 at neck shaping leaving ends long. Sew ends of rows on back of Head & Body together. Stuff and shape. Pull ends of yarn at neck tight to gather and shape neck. Tie in knot to secure. Tuck ends inside Body. Continue to shape Head and Body with fiberfill.

For **ear** (make 2), with J hook and cream, ch 4, 9 dc in fourth ch from hook. Leaving long end for sewing, fasten off.

Sew to top Head 1" apart.

MUZZLE

Row 1: With tan, ch 20, draw up lp in second ch from hook, draw up lp in each ch across, turn. *(20 lps on hook)*

Row 2: With cream, work lps off hook, **do not turn.**

Row 3: Ch 1, skip first vertical bar, draw up lp in each vertical bar across, turn.

Row 4: With tan, work lps off hook, **do not turn.** At end of last row, fasten off.

Row 5: For **nose,** join black with sl st in first

vertical bar, ch 1, draw up lp in each vertical bar across, **do not turn,** yo, draw through all lps on hook to gather, ch 1. Fasten off.

Sew ends of rows together. Sew Muzzle to front of Head stuffing before closing *(see photo)*.

For **eyes,** with Black, using French knot *(see illustration),* embroider eyes centered above Muzzle ¼" apart. Tie ribbon into bow around Bear's neck.

French Knot (2-wrap)

ARM (make 2)

Row 1: With tan, ch 12, draw up lp in second ch from hook, draw up lp in each ch across, turn. *(12 lps on hook)*

Row 2: With cream, work lps off hook, **do not turn.**

Row 3: Ch 1, skip first vertical bar, draw up lp in each vertical bar across, turn.

Row 4: With tan, work lps off hook, **do not turn.**

Row 5: Ch 1, skip first vertical bar, draw up lp in each vertical bar across, turn.

Rows 6-31: Repeat rows 2-5 consecutively, ending with row 3. At end of last row, **do not turn,** yo, draw through all lps on hook to gather end of paw, ch 1. Fasten off.

Sew ends of rows together. Stuff.

Sew Arms to each side of Body below neck as shown in photo. Tack top of Arms to Body.

LEG (make 2)

Row 1: With tan, ch 16, draw up lp in second ch from hook, draw up lp in each ch across, turn. *(16 lps on hook)*

Row 2: With cream, work lps off hook, **do not turn.**

Row 3: Ch 1, skip first vertical bar, draw up lp in each vertical bar across, turn.

Row 4: With tan, work lps off hook, **do not turn.**

Row 5: Ch 1, skip first vertical bar, draw up lp in each vertical bar across, turn.

Rows 6-28: Repeat rows 2-5 consecutively, ending with row 4.

Row 29: For **foot shaping,** ch 1, skip first vertical bar, draw up lp in each of next 3 vertical bars, draw up lp in top strand of next horizontal bar, (draw up lp in next vertical bar, draw up lp in top strand of next horizontal bar) 9 times, draw up lp in each of last 3 vertical bars, turn. *(26 lps on hook)*

Rows 30-35: Repeat rows 2-5 consecutively, ending with row 3. At end of last row, **do not turn,** yo, draw through all lps on hook, ch 1. Fasten off.

Sew ends of rows together. Stuff.

Flatten last rnd and sew Legs to bottom of Body spaced 1½" apart.♦

Heart Puffs

continued from page 57

draw up lp in top strand of next 7 horizontal bars, puff st, draw up lp in top strand of last 11 horizontal bars, turn.

Row 34: With white, work lps off hook, **do not turn.**

Row 35: Repeat row 33.

Row 36: With pink, work lps off hook, **do not turn.**

Row 37: Ch 1, skip first vertical bar, draw up lp in top strand of next 8 horizontal bars, puff st, (draw up lp in top strand of next 5 horizontal bars, puff st) 2 times, draw up lp in top strand of last 9 horizontal bars, turn.

Row 38: With white, work lps off hook, **do not turn.**

Row 39: Repeat row 37.

Row 40: With pink, work lps off hook, **do not turn.**

Row 41: Repeat row 37.

Row 42: With white, work lps off hook, **do not turn.**

Row 43: Repeat row 37.

Row 44: With pink, work lps off hook, **do not turn.**

Row 45: Ch 1, skip first vertical bar, draw up lp in top strand of next 10 horizontal bars, (puff st, draw up lp in top strand of next horizontal bar, puff st), draw up lp in top strand of next 3 horizontal bars; repeat between ( ), draw up lp in top strand of last 11 horizontal bars, turn.

Row 46: With white, work lps off hook, **do not turn.**

Row 47: Repeat row 45.

Row 48: With pink, work lps off hook, **do not turn.**

Row 49: Ch 1, skip first vertical bar, draw up lp in top strand of each horizontal bar across, turn.

Row 50: With white, work lps off hook, **do not turn.**

Row 51: Ch 1, skip first vertical bar, draw up lp in top strand of each horizontal bar across, turn.

Rows 52-56: Repeat rows 48-51 consecutively, ending with row 48.

Rows 57-328: Repeat rows 5-56 consecutively, ending with row 16.

Row 329: Ch 1, sl st in each vertical bar across. Fasten off.

Edging

Rnd 1: Working around outer edge, with predominantly pink side facing you, using F hook for remainder of pattern, join pink with sc in first st of last row, 2 sc in same st, ch 1, skip next st, (sc in next st, ch 1, skip next st) across to last st, 3 sc in last st; *working in ends of rows, skip first pink stripe, (sc in next white stripe, ch 1, skip next pink stripe) across*; working in starting ch on opposite side of row 1, 3 sc in first ch, ch 1, skip next ch, (sc in next ch, ch 1, skip next ch) across to last ch, 3 sc in last ch; repeat between **, join with sl st in first sc. Fasten off.

Rnd 2: Join white with sc in any center corner st, 2 sc in same st, ch 1, skip next sc, (sc in next ch sp, ch 1, skip next sc) across to next center corner st, *3 sc in next corner st, ch 1, skip next sc, (sc in next ch sp, ch 1, skip next sc) across to next center corner st; repeat from * around, join. Fasten off.

Rnd 3: With pink, repeat rnd 2.

Rnd 4: Repeat rnd 2.

Assembly

Holding two Panels wrong sides together, with hearts aligned in same direction, join pink with sl st in center corner st at bottom of first Panel, ch 1, sl st in center corner st at bottom of second Panel, (ch 1, sl st in next st or ch sp on first Panel, ch 1, sl st in next st or ch sp on second Panel) across. Fasten off.

Join remaining Panels in same manner.

BORDER

Working around entire outer edge of Afghan, join pink with sc in any center corner st; for **picot,** ch 3, sl st in third ch from hook; skip next sc, (sl st in next ch sp, picot, skip next sc) across to next center corner st, *sc in next corner st, picot, skip next sc, (sl st in next ch sp, picot, skip next sc) across to next center corner st; repeat from * around, join with sl st in first sc. Fasten off.♦

Sunny Scallops

Designed by Mary Ann Sipes

Colors of soft, golden sunlight and puffy, white clouds are worked together in a pretty scalloped design that makes a heavenly pattern on either side!

SIZE: 33" x 47".

MATERIALS: 3-ply pompadour sport yarn—14 oz. yellow and 7 oz. white; G double-ended swivel hook and F hook or hook size needed to obtain gauge.

GAUGES: With **double-ended hook,** 4 sts = 1"; 4 pattern rows = 1".

SPECIAL STITCHES: For **sc lp,** insert hook in next st, yo, pull lp through, ch 1.

For **dc lp,** yo, insert hook in next st, yo, pull lp through, yo, pull through 2 lps on hook.

For **scallop,** 5 dc lps under next horizontal bar.

NOTES: Read General Instructions on page 6 before beginning pattern.

Use double-ended hook unless otherwise stated.

AFGHAN

Row 1: With yellow, ch 120, draw up lp in second ch from hook, draw up lp in each ch across, turn. *(120 lps on hook)*

Row 2: With white, work lps off hook, **do not turn.**

Row 3: Ch 1, skip first vertical bar, **sc lp** *(see Special Stitches)* under each **horizontal bar** *(see illustration)* across, turn.

Horizontal Bar

Row 4: With yellow, work lps off hook, **do not turn.**

Row 5: Ch 2 *(counts as first dc lp),* **dc lp** *(see Special Stitches)* in first vertical bar, skip next 4

horizontal bars, (**scallop** under next horizontal bar—*see Special Stitches,* skip next 4 horizontal bars) across to last vertical bar, 2 dc lps in last vertical bar, turn. *(23 scallops, 4 dc lps)*

Row 6: With white, work lps off hook, **do not turn.**

Row 7: Ch 1, skip first vertical bar, sc lp under each horizontal bar across to last vertical bar, sc lp in last vertical bar, turn.

Rows 8-176: Repeat rows 4-7 consecutively, ending with row 4.

Row 177: Ch 1, skip first vertical bar, sl st in each vertical bar across. Fasten off.

BORDER

Rnd 1: Working around outer edge, with F hook, join yellow with sl st in first st of last row, ch 3 *(counts as first dc),* 8 dc in same st, *skip next st, sc in next st, skip next 2 sts, (5 dc in next st, skip next 2 sts, sc in next st, skip next 2 sts) across to last st, 9 dc in last st; working in ends of rows, skip next white row, sc in next yellow row, skip next white row, (5 dc in next yellow row, skip next white row, sc in next yellow row, skip next white row) across*; working in starting ch on opposite side of row 1, 9 dc in first ch; repeat between **, join with sl st in top of ch-3. Fasten off.

Rnd 2: With F hook, join white with sc in third st of first 9-dc corner, [◊(ch 2, skip next st, sc in next st) 2 times, (dc, ch 2, dc) in next sc, *sc in center st of next 5-dc group, (dc, ch 2, dc) in next sc; repeat from * across◊ to next 9-dc corner, sc in third st of next 9-dc corner]; repeat between [ ] 2 more times; repeat between ◊◊, join with sl st in first sc. Fasten off.

Rnd 3: With F hook, join yellow with sl st in first sc, (ch 3, 4 dc) in same st, sc in next ch sp, skipping dc (5 dc in next sc, sc in next ch sp) around, join with sl st in top of ch-3. Fasten off.♦

Dino-snore Pillow

DESIGNED BY DEBBIE TABOR

Make-believe adventures in the long-ago land of dinosaurs come to life with this cuddly-sweet, and not at all ferocious, playtime pal!

SIZE: 16½" x 25½".

MATERIALS: Worsted yarn—5 oz. each med. blue and variegated, small amount each lt. teal, black and white; polyester fiberfill; tapestry needle; J double-ended and J hooks or hook size needed to obtain gauge.

GAUGE: With **double-ended hook,** 4 sts = 1"; 6 rows = 1".

NOTES: Read General Instructions on page 6 before beginning pattern.

Use double-ended hook unless otherwise stated.

FIRST BODY SIDE

Row 1: Starting at bottom, with med. blue, ch 90, draw up lp in second ch from hook, draw up lp in each ch across, turn. *(90 lps on hook)*

Row 2: With variegated, work lps off hook, **do not turn.**

Row 3: Ch 1, skip first vertical bar, draw up lp in top strand of each **horizontal bar** across *(see illustration),* turn.

Horizontal Bar

Row 4: With med. blue, work lps off hook across to last 3 lps on hook, yo, draw through last 3 lps on hook, **do not turn.** *(counts as one vertical bar).*

Row 5: Ch 1, skip first vertical bar, draw up lp in top strand of each horizontal bar across, turn. *(89 lps on hook)*

Row 6: With variegated, draw through first 2 lps on hook *(counts as one vertical bar on next row),* (yo, draw through 2 lps on hook) across, **do not turn.**

Row 7: Ch 1, skip first vertical bar, draw up lp in top strand of each horizontal bar across, turn. *(88 lps on hook)*

Rows 8-27: Repeat rows 4-7 consecutively, ending with *78 lps on hook* in last row.

Row 28: With med. blue, draw through first 2 lps on hook, (yo, draw through 2 lps on hook) across to last 3 lps on hook, yo, draw through last 3 lps on hook, **do not turn.**

Row 29: Ch 1, skip first vertical bar, draw up lp in top strand of each horizontal bar across, turn. *(76 lps on hook)*

Row 30: With variegated, repeat row 28.

Row 31: Ch 1, skip first vertical bar, draw up lp in top strand of each horizontal bar across, turn. *(74 lps on hook)*

Rows 32-35: Repeat rows 28-31, ending with *70 lps on hook* in last row.

Row 36: With med. blue, draw

through first 2 lps on hook, yo, draw through 3 lps on hook, (yo, draw through 2 lps on hook) across to last 3 lps on hook, yo, draw through last 3 lps on hook, **do not turn.**

Row 37: Ch 1, skip first vertical bar, draw up lp in top strand of each horizontal bar across, turn. *(67 lps on hook)*

Rows 38-39: With variegated, repeat rows 28-29. *(65 lps on hook)*

Rows 40-41: Repeat rows 28 and 29. *(63 lps on hook)*

Row 42: With variegated, draw through first 2 lps on hook, (yo, draw through 2 lps on hook) across, **do not turn.**

Row 43: Ch 1, skip first vertical bar, draw up lp in top strand of each horizontal bar across, turn. *(62 lps on hook)*

Rows 44-45: Repeat rows 28 and 29, ending with *60 lps on hook* in last row.

Rows 46-47: Repeat rows 42 and 43, ending with *59 lps on hook* in last row.

Rows 48-49: With med. blue, repeat rows 42 and 43, ending with *58 lps on hook* in last row.

Row 50: With variegated, draw through first 2 lps on hook, (yo, draw through 2 lps on hook) across to last 3 lps on hook, yo, draw through last 3 lps on hook, **do not turn.**

Row 51: Ch 1, skip first vertical bar, draw up lp in top strand of each horizontal bar across, turn. *(56 lps on hook)*

Rows 52-53: With med. blue, repeat rows 50 and 51, ending with *54 lps on hook* in last row.

Rows 54-55: Repeat rows 50 and 51, ending with *52 lps on hook* in last row.

Row 56: With med. blue, draw through first 2 lps on hook, yo, draw through 3 lps on hook, (yo, draw through 2 lps on hook) across to last 3 lps on hook, yo, draw through last 3 lps on hook, **do not turn.**

Row 57: Ch 1, skip first vertical bar, draw up lp in top strand of next 39 horizontal bars, sl st in top strand of last 9 horizontal bars. *(40 lps on hook)*

Row 58: With variegated, draw through first 2 lps on hook, (yo, draw through 2 lps on hook) across, **do not turn.**

Row 59: Ch 1, skip first vertical bar, draw up lp in top strand of each horizontal bar across, turn. *(39 lps on hook)*

Rows 60-61: With med. blue, repeat rows 58 and 59, ending with *38 lps on hook* in last row.

Rows 62-63: Repeat rows 50 and 51, ending with *36 lps on hook* in last row.

Rows 64-65: With med. blue, repeat rows 50 and 51, ending with *34 lps on hook* in last row.

Rows 66-67: Repeat rows 50 and 51, ending with *32 lps on hook* in last row.

Row 68: With med. blue, draw through first 2 lps on hook, yo, draw through 3 lps on hook, (yo, draw through 2 lps on hook) across to last 5 lps on hook, (yo, draw through 3 lps on hook) 2 times, **do not turn.**

Row 69: Ch 1, skip first vertical bar, draw up lp in top strand of each horizontal bar across, turn. *(28 lps on hook)*

Row 70: With variegated, draw through first 2 lps on hook, yo, draw through 3 lps on hook, (yo, draw through 2 lps on hook) across to last 7 lps on hook, (yo, draw through 3 lps on hook) 3 times, **do not turn.**

Row 71: Ch 1, skip first vertical bar, draw up lp in top strand of each horizontal bar across, turn. *(23 lps on hook)*

Row 72: With med. blue, draw through first 2 lps on hook, (yo, draw through 3 lps on hook) 2 times, (yo, draw through 2 lps on hook) across to last 7 lps on hook, (yo, draw through 3 lps on hook) 3 times, **do not turn.**

Row 73: Ch 1, skip first vertical bar, sl st in top strand of each horizontal bar across. Fasten off. *(17 sl sts)*

SECOND BODY SIDE

Reversing colors, work same as First Body Side on page 65.

LEG (make 4)

Row 1: With med. blue, ch 13, draw up lp in second ch from hook, draw up lp in each ch across, turn. *(13 lps on hook)*

Row 2: With variegated, work lps off hook, **do not turn.**

Row 3: Ch 1, skip first vertical bar, draw up lp in top strand of each horizontal bar across, turn.

Row 4: With med. blue, work lps off hook, **do not turn.**

Row 5: Ch 1, skip first vertical bar, draw up lp

in top strand of each horizontal bar across, turn.

Rows 6-12: Repeat rows 2-5 consecutively, ending with row 4.

Row 13: For **foot shaping,** ch 5, draw up lp in second ch from hook, draw up lp in next 3 chs, draw up lp in top strand of each horizontal bar across, turn. *(17 lps on hook)*

Rows 14-40: Repeat rows 2-5 consecutively, ending with row 4.

Row 41: Ch 1, skip first vertical bar, sl st in top strand of next 4 horizontal bars, draw up lp in top strand of each horizontal bar across, turn. *(13 lps on hook)*

Rows 42-52: Repeat rows 2-5 consecutively, ending with row 4.

Row 53: Ch 1, skip first vertical bar, sl st in top strand of each horizontal bar across. Fasten off.

Fold Leg in half crosswise, matching ends of rows and foot shaping, sew together stuffing before closing.

HORN (make 3)

NOTE: Do not join or turn unless otherwise stated. Mark first st of each rnd.

Rnd 1: With J hook and med. blue, ch 4, sl st in first ch to form ring, ch 1, sc in each ch around, **do not join.** *(4 sc made)*

Rnd 2: Working this rnd in **back lps** only (see page 11), sc in each st around.

Rnd 3: (Sc in next st, 2 sc in next st) around. *(6)*

Rnds 4-6: Sc in each st around.

Rnd 7: (Sc in next st, 2 sc in next st) around. *(9)*

Rnds 8-9: Sc in each st around. At end of last rnd, join with sl st in first sc. Fasten off.

ASSEMBLY

1: Holding Body Sides with predominantly blue sides together, matching sts, with variegated, sew together stuffing before closing.

2: Sew two Legs with foot facing forward to row 6 on each Body Side about 9" from tip of tail *(sharply angled end)*. Sew other two Legs in same manner spaced about 1" in front of back Legs *(see photo)*.

3: Stuff Horns lightly. Sew one Horn over rows 24-30 centered over seam on front of nose. Sew remaining Horns to top of head spaced about 1" apart.

COLLAR

Row 1: Working across Body from side to side, with J hook and variegated, join with sc in st on row 23 about 6" from center front seam below nose *(see photo)*, sc in next 4 sts; working vertically, evenly space 33 sts across to row 23 on other side, sc in next 5 sts of row 23 being sure to end last st about 6" from center front seam, turn. *(43 sc made)*

Row 2: Ch 2 *(counts as first hdc)*, hdc in each st across, turn. Fasten off.

Row 3: With J hook, join med. blue with sl st in first st, (ch 2, dc, tr, dc, hdc) in same st, *sc in next st, (hdc, dc, tr, dc, hdc) in next st; repeat from * across. Fasten off.

FINISHING

1: For **tail shaping,** with tapestry needle and variegated, working through all thicknesses and pulling stitches slightly snug to form shaping at base of tail, stitch a line from bottom seam just behind back Legs up 2" toward top seam.

2: Using stitches and colors shown in illustration, embroider eyes over rows 34-42, placing eyelid 1" from center front seam.

3: For **mouth shaping,** tuck bottom corner on tip of nose to inside; tack in place.♦

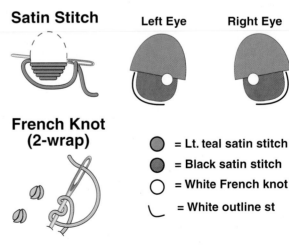

Satin Stitch   Left Eye   Right Eye

French Knot (2-wrap)

● = Lt. teal satin stitch
● = Black satin stitch
○ = White French knot
◡ = White outline st

Outline Stitch

Gingham Patch

Designed by Mary Ann Sipes

Cozy textured blocks arranged in reverse-color order and finished with alternate-color edgings create a charming gingham pattern that's as pretty as a picture!

SIZE: 41" square.

MATERIALS: 3-ply pompadour sport yarn—16 oz. each lavender and white; G double-ended swivel and F hooks or hook size needed to obtain gauge.

GAUGE: With **double-ended hook,** 2 sts and 2 ch sps = 1"; 8 rows = 1".

SPECIAL STITCHES: For **puff stitch (puff st),** yo, insert hook in specified st, yo, draw up lp, yo, insert hook in same st, yo, draw up lp, yo, draw through 5 lps on hook.

For **shell,** (puff st, ch 3, puff st) in next st.

NOTES: Read General Instructions on page 6 before beginning pattern.

Use double-ended hook unless otherwise stated.

BLOCK (make 49)

Row 1: With white, ch 16, draw up lp in second ch from hook, yo, draw up lp in same ch, (skip next ch, draw up lp in next ch, yo, draw up lp in same ch) across, turn. *(25 lps on hook)*

Row 2: With lavender, draw through one lp on hook, (ch 1, yo, draw through 4 lps on hook) across, **do not turn.**

Row 3: Ch 1, (draw up lp in next ch sp, yo, draw up lp in same sp) across, turn.

Row 4: With white, repeat row 2.

Row 5: Ch 1, draw up lp in next ch sp, yo, draw up lp in same sp) across, turn.

Rows 6-32: Repeat rows 2-5 consecutively, ending with row 4. At end of last row, fasten off.

EDGING A

Rnd 1: Working in ch sps and in ends of rows around outer edge, evenly spacing sts so piece lays flat, with predominantly white side of one Block facing you, using F hook and lavender, join with sl st in any corner, ch 1 *(does not count as a st),* (**puff st**—*see Special Stitches,* ch 3, puff st) in same sp, ch 1, evenly sp (puff st, ch 1) 7 times across to next corner, *****shell *(see Special Stitches)* in next corner, ch 1, evenly sp (puff st, ch 1) 7 times across ends of rows or sts; repeat from * around, join with sl st in top of first puff st. *(9 puff sts and 8 ch-1 sps across each side between corner ch sps)*

Rnd 2: Ch 1, 5 sc in each corner ch sp and 2 sc in each ch-1 sp around, join with sl st in first sc. Fasten off. *(16 sc across each side between 5-sc corners)*

Repeat around 24 more Blocks ending with a total of 25 Blocks with Edging A.

EDGING B

With predominantly lavender side of one Block facing you, using white, work same as Edging A.

Repeat around 23 more Blocks ending with a total of 24 Blocks with Edging B.

ASSEMBLY

With wrong sides held together, matching sts and alternating Blocks with Edging A and Edging B, with lavender, sew together through **back lps** *(see Stitch Guide on page 11)* in seven rows of seven Blocks each.

BORDER

Rnd 1: Working around entire outer edge of Blocks, using F hook on remainder of pattern, join white with sl st in center st of any 5-sc corner, ch 1, (puff st, ch 3, puff st, ch 3, puff st) in same st *(corner made),* [◊(skip next st, sc in next st, skip next st, shell in next st) 5 times, *sc in next seam, skip next st, shell in next st, (skip next st, sc in next st, skip next st, shell in next st) 4 times, skip next 2 sts; repeat from * 4 more times, sc in next

continued on page 73

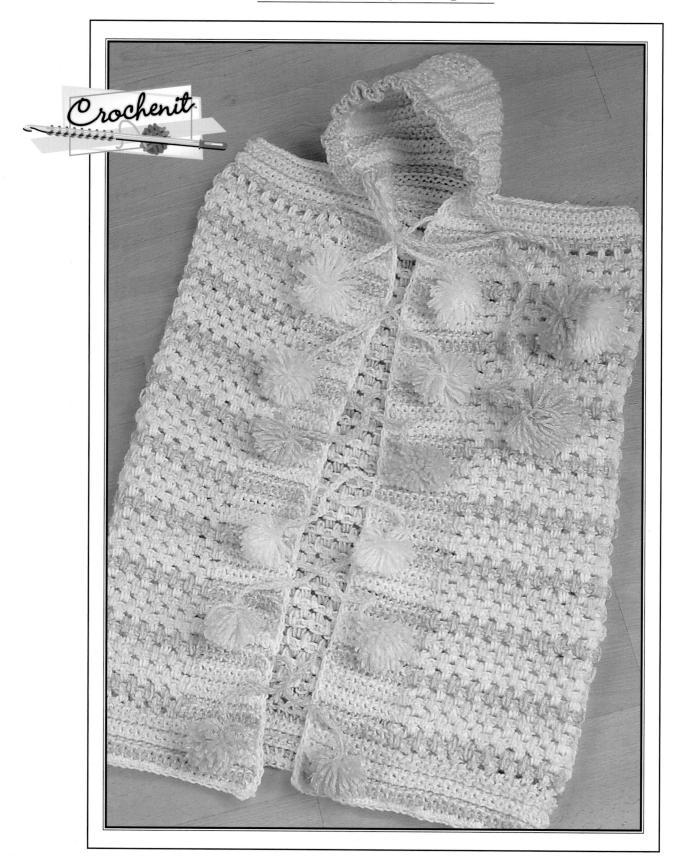

Pompom Baby Bunting

DESIGNED BY MELINDA WIGINGTON

Baby will be snug as a bug in this adorable bunting that fastens up easily with ties of fuzzy-soft pompoms!

SIZE: Fits infant up to 6 months.

MATERIALS: Baby pompadour yarn—9 oz. white, 6 oz. each blue, green and yellow; 4" square piece of cardboard; 2½" square piece of cardboard; tapestry needle; Crochenit™ and K hooks or hook size needed to obtain gauge.

GAUGE: With **Crochenit™ hook,** 4 shells = 2"; 10 rows = 2".

NOTES: Read General Instructions on page 8 before beginning pattern.

Use Crochenit™ hook unless otherwise stated.

BODY

Row 1: With white, ch 110, draw up lp in second ch from hook, draw up lp in each ch across, turn. *(110 lps on hook)*

Row 2: With blue, work lps off hook, **do not turn.**

Row 3: Ch 1, skip first vertical bar, draw up lp in each vertical bar across, turn.

Rows 4-12: Working in color sequence of white, yellow, white, green, repeat rows 2 and 3 alternately, ending with row 2 and white.

Row 13: Ch 1, skip first vertical bar, draw up lp in each of next 10 vertical bars, for **pattern st,** draw up lp under next **horizontal bar** *(see illustration),* yo, draw up lp in same sp, (skip next horizontal bar, draw up lp

Horizontal Bar

under next horizontal bar, yo, draw up lp in same sp) 44 times, draw up lp in each of last 11 vertical bars, turn. *(45 pattern sts)*

Row 14: With blue, work off first 11 lps on hook, *ch 1, yo, draw through 4 lps on hook *(ch sp and shell completed);* repeat from * 44 more times, ch 1, work last 11 lps off hook, **do not turn.** *(46 ch sps)*

Row 15: Ch 1, skip first vertical bar, draw up lp in each of next 10 vertical bars, (draw up lp in next ch sp, yo, draw up lp in same sp) 46 times, draw up lp in each of last 11 vertical bars, turn. *(46 pattern sts)*

Row 16: With white, work off first 11 lps on hook, *yo, draw through 4 lps on hook *(shell completed)*; repeat from * 45 more times, work last 11 lps off hook, **do not turn.**

Row 17: Ch 1, skip first vertical bar, draw up lp in each of next 10 vertical bars, draw up lp in sp between first 2 shells, yo, draw up lp in same sp, (draw up lp in next sp between shells, yo, draw up lp in same sp) 44 times, draw up lp in each of last 11 vertical bars, turn. *(45 pattern sts)*

Rows 18-122: Working in color sequence of yellow, white, green, white, blue, white, repeat rows 14-17 consecutively, ending with row 14 and blue.

Row 123: Ch 1, skip first vertical bar, draw up lp in each of next 10 vertical bars, draw up lp in next ch sp, (yo, draw up lp in next ch sp) 43 times, draw up lp in each of next 2 ch sps, draw up lp in each of last 11 vertical bars, turn. *(111 lps on hook)*

Rows 124-132: Working in color sequence of white, yellow, white, green, repeat rows 2 and 3 alternately, ending with row 2 and white.

Row 133: Ch 1, skip first vertical bar, sl st in each vertical bar across. Fasten off. *(110 sl sts)*

HOOD

Row 1: Join blue with sl st in first sl st, ch 1, draw up lp in each of next 7 sts; for **first shoulder,** skip next 39 sts; draw up lp in each of next 16 sts; for **second shoulder,** skip next 39 sts; draw up lp in each of last 8 sts, **do not turn.** *(32 lps on hook)*

Row 2: With blue, work lps off hook, **do not turn.**

Row 3: Ch 1, skip first vertical bar, draw up lp in each vertical bar across, turn.

Row 4: With white, work lps off hook, **do not turn.**

Row 5: Ch 1, skip first vertical bar, draw up lp in each vertical bar across, turn.

Rows 6-14: Working in color sequence of yellow, white, green, white, blue, repeat rows 4 and 5 alternately, ending with row 4 and blue.

Row 15: Ch 1, skip first vertical bar, draw up lp in each of next 14 vertical bars, (draw up lp under next horizontal bar, draw up lp in next vertical bar) 3 times, draw up lp in each of last 14 verti-cal bars, turn. *(35 lps on hook)*

Row 16: With white, work lps off hook, **do not turn.**

Row 17: Ch 1, skip first vertical bar, draw up lp in each of next 16 vertical bars, (draw up lp under next horizontal bar, draw up lp in next vertical bar) 2 times, draw up lp in each of last 16 vertical bars, turn. *(37 lps on hook)*

Row 18: With yellow, work lps off hook, **do not turn.**

Row 19: Ch 1, skip first vertical bar, draw up lp in each of next 17 vertical bars, (draw up lp under next horizontal bar, draw up lp in next vertical bar) 2 times, draw up lp in each of last 17 vertical bars, turn. *(39 lps on hook)*

Row 20: With white, work lps off hook, **do not turn.**

Row 21: Ch 1, skip first vertical bar, draw up lp in each of next 18 vertical bars, (draw up lp under next horizontal bar, draw up lp in next vertical bar) 2 times, draw up lp in each of last 18 vertical bars, turn. *(41 lps on hook)*

Row 22: With green, work lps off hook, **do not turn.**

Row 23: Ch 1, skip first vertical bar, draw up lp in each of next 19 vertical bars, (draw up under next horizontal bar, draw up lp in next vertical bar) 2 times, draw up lp in each of last 19 vertical bars, turn. *(43 lps on hook)*

Row 24: With white, work lps off hook, **do not turn.**

Row 25: Ch 1, skip first vertical bar, draw up lp in each vertical bar across, turn.

Rows 26-32: Working in color sequence of blue, white, yellow, white, repeat rows 24 and 25 alternately, ending with row 24 and white.

Row 33: Ch 1, sl st in each vertical bar across. Fasten off.

CROWN

Row 1: With white, ch 8, draw up lp in second ch from hook, draw up lp in each ch across, turn. *(8 lps on hook)*

Row 2: With blue, work lps off hook, **do not turn.**

Row 3: Ch 1, skip first vertical bar, draw up lp in each vertical bar across, turn.

Rows 4-30: Working in color sequence of

white, yellow, white, green, white, blue, repeat rows 2 and 3 alternately, ending with row 2 and yellow.

Row 31: Ch 1, sl st in each vertical bar across. Fasten off.

For **first side trim,** working in ends of rows across one long edge, with K hook and white, join with sc in row 1, evenly space 15 more sc across. Fasten off.

For **second side trim,** working in ends of rows on other long edge, with K hook and white, join with sc in last row, evenly space 15 more sc across. Fasten off.

Matching light sides and dark sides on Hood; easing to fit, sew ends of rows and starting ch of Crown to last row on Hood.

For **shoulder seams,** flatten last row of Bunting on one side of Hood, working through both thicknesses, sl st together.

Repeat on other shoulder.

EDGING

Working around entire outer edge, in ends of rows, in sts and in chs, with K hook and white, join with sc in row 2 *(this is the first blue row)* on Bunting, sc evenly spaced around with 3 sc in each bottom corner, join with sl st in first sc. Fasten off.

HOOD TRIM

For **ruffle,** with K hook and blue, join with sl st in st on Edging at base of Hood, (ch 3, dc) in same st, 2 dc in each st across to opposite side of Hood leaving remaining sts unworked. Fasten off.

For **pompom** (make 2), wrap yellow around 4" cardboard 50 times, then wrap blue around cardboard 50 times; slide all loops off cardboard, tie separate strand blue around center of all strands; cut loops. Trim ends.

For **tie,** with K hook and one strand each blue and yellow held together, ch 110. Fasten off.

Weave tie through sts of Edging across bottom of Hood ruffle, sew one pompom to each end.

FASTENER (make 4 each yellow, green and blue)

For **pompom,** wrap yarn around 2½" cardboard 50 times; slide loops off cardboard, tie a separate strand of same-color yarn around center of all strands; cut loops. Trim ends.

For **tie,** using K hook, ch 20. Fasten off.

Sew one pompom to each matching tie.

Working in color sequence of yellow, green, blue, sew six ties evenly spaced down left front. Matching colors of ties on left front, repeat on right front.♦

Gingham Patch

continued from page 69

seam, skip next st, shell in next st, (skip next st, sc in next st, skip next st, shell in next st) 4 times, skip next st, sc in next st◊, (puff st, ch 3, puff st, ch 3, puff st) in next st]; repeat between [ ] 2 more times; repeat between ◊◊, join with sl st in top of first puff st. Fasten off. *(36 sc and 35 ch sps across each side between puff st corners)*

Rnd 2: Join lavender with sl st in any center corner puff st, ch 1, (puff st, ch 3, puff st) in same sp, [◊sc in next ch sp, *(puff st, ch 3, puff st) in next sc, sc in next ch sp; repeat from * across◊ to next center corner puff st, (puff st, ch 3, puff st) in corner puff st]; repeat between [ ] 2 more times; repeat between ◊◊, join. Fasten off.

Rnd 3: Join white with sc in any corner ch sp, (puff st, ch 3, puff st) in next sc, *sc in next ch sp, (puff st, ch 3, puff st) in next sc; repeat from * around, join with sl st in first sc. Fasten off.

Rnd 4: Join lavender with sl st in any corner sc, ch 1, (puff st, ch 3, puff st, ch 3, puff st) in same st, [◊sc in next ch sp, *(puff st, ch 3, puff st) in next sc, sc in next ch sp; repeat from * across◊ to next corner sc, (puff st, ch 3, puff st, ch 3, puff st) in next sc]; repeat between [ ] 2 more times; repeat between ◊◊, join with sl st in top of first puff st. Fasten off.♦

Dandy Diamonds

DESIGNED BY MARY ANN SIPES

Cozy panels of dimensional diamonds add texture and warmth to this jewel of an afghan that sparkles in baby pompadour yarn!

SIZE: 34½" x 46".

MATERIALS: Baby pompadour yarn—18½ oz. white and 12 oz. blue; G double-ended and F hooks or hook size needed to obtain gauge.

GAUGE: With **double-ended hook,** 4 sts = 1"; 9 rows = 1".

NOTES: Read General Instructions on page 6 before beginning pattern.

Use double-ended hook unless otherwise stated.

PANEL A (make 3)

Row 1: With white, ch 24, draw up lp in second ch from hook, draw up lp in each ch across, turn. *(24 lps on hook)*

Row 2: With blue, draw through one lp on hook, (yo, draw through 2 lps on hook) 11 times, ch 3, (yo, draw through 2 lps on hook) across, **do not turn.**

Note: Push ch-3 to front of each row throughout. Blue ch-3's will show on white side; white ch-3's will show on blue side.

Row 3: Ch 1, skip first vertical bar, draw up lp in each vertical bar across, turn.

Row 4: With white, repeat row 2.

Row 5: Ch 1, skip first vertical bar, draw up lp in each vertical bar across, turn.

Row 6: With blue, draw through one lp on hook, (yo, draw through 2 lps on hook) 10 times, ch 3, (yo, draw through 2 lps on hook) 2 times, ch 3, (yo, draw through 2 lps on hook) across, **do not turn.**

Row 7: Ch 1, skip first vertical bar, draw up lp in each vertical bar across, turn.

Row 8: With white, repeat row 6.

Row 9: Ch 1, skip first vertical bar, draw up lp in each vertical bar across, turn.

Row 10: With blue, draw through one lp on hook, (yo, draw through 2 lps on hook) 9 times, ch 3, *(yo, draw through 2 lps on hook) 2 times, ch 3; repeat from * one more time, (yo, draw through 2 lps on hook) across, **do not turn.**

Row 11: Ch 1, skip first vertical bar, draw up lp in each vertical bar across, turn.

Row 12: With white, repeat row 10.

Row 13: Ch 1, skip first vertical bar, draw up lp in each vertical bar across, turn.

Row 14: With blue, draw through one lp on hook, (yo, draw through 2 lps on hook) 8 times, ch 3, *(yo, draw through 2 lps on hook) 2 times, ch 3; repeat from * 2 more times, (yo, draw through 2 lps on hook) across, **do not turn.**

Row 15: Ch 1, skip first vertical bar, draw up lp in each vertical bar across, turn.

Row 16: With white, repeat row 14.

Row 17: Ch 1, skip first vertical bar, draw up lp in each vertical bar across, turn.

Row 18: With blue, draw through one lp on hook, (yo, draw through 2 lps on hook) 7 times, ch 3, *(yo, draw through 2 lps on hook) 2 times, ch 3; repeat from * 3 more times, (yo, draw through 2 lps on hook) across, **do not turn.**

Row 19: Ch 1, skip first vertical bar, draw up lp in each vertical bar across, turn.

Row 20: With white, repeat row 18.

Row 21: Ch 1, skip first vertical bar, draw up lp in each vertical bar across, turn.

Row 22: Repeat row 14.

Row 23: Ch 1, skip first vertical bar, draw up lp in each vertical bar across, turn.

Row 24: With white, repeat row 14.

Row 25: Ch 1, skip first vertical bar, draw up lp in each vertical bar across, turn.

Row 26: Repeat row 10.

Row 27: Ch 1, skip first vertical bar, draw up lp in each vertical bar across, turn.

Row 28: With white, repeat row 10.

Row 29: Ch 1, skip first vertical bar, draw up lp in each vertical bar across, turn.

continued on page 78

Baby Blocks

DESIGNED BY DEBBIE TABOR

These cuddly-soft toys are easy for little fingers to grab and safe to play with. Three different designs help baby learn about colors and shapes!

SIZES: Square Block is 3" square; Triangle Block is 3" tall; Round Block is 2½" tall x 3½" wide.

MATERIALS FOR ONE OF EACH:
Worsted yarn—1½ oz. each lime, yellow, blue, teal, bright pink and dk. pink; polyester fiberfill; tapestry needle; G double-ended hook or hook size needed to obtain gauge.

GAUGE: 5 sts = 1"; 10 rows = 1".

NOTE: Read General Instructions on page 6 before beginning pattern.

SQUARE BLOCK
Side (make 6)

Row 1: With bright pink, ch 15, draw up lp in second ch from hook, draw up lp in each ch across, turn. *(15 lps on hook)*

Row 2: With dk. pink, work lps off hook, **do not turn.**

Row 3: Ch 1, skip first vertical bar, draw up lp in top strand of each **horizontal bar** across *(see illustration),* turn.

Horizontal Bar

Row 4: With bright pink, work lps off hook, **do not turn.**

Row 5: Ch 1, skip first vertical bar, draw up lp in top strand of each horizontal bar across, turn.

Rows 6-28: Repeat rows 2-5 consecutively, ending with row 4. At end of last row, fasten off.

Sew pieces together forming a square, stuffing before closing.

TRIANGLE BLOCK
Side (make 3)

Row 1: With blue, ch 15, draw up lp in second ch from hook, draw up lp in each ch across, turn. *(15 lps on hook)*

Row 2: With teal, work lps off hook, **do not turn.**

Row 3: Ch 1, skip first vertical bar, draw up lp in top strand of each horizontal bar across, turn.

Row 4: With blue, work lps off hook, **do not turn.**

Row 5: Ch 1, skip first vertical bar, sl st in top strand of next horizontal bar, draw up lp in top strand of each horizontal bar across to last hori-

zontal bar, sl st in top strand of last horizontal bar, turn. *(13 lps on hook)*

Rows 6-28: Repeat rows 2-5 consecutively, ending with row 4 and 3 lps on hook.

Row 29: Ch 1, sl st in top strand of each horizontal bar across. Fasten off.

Sew ends of rows of three Sides together leaving bottom open.

Base

Row 1: With blue, ch 15, draw up lp in second ch from hook, draw up lp in each ch across, turn. *(15 lps on hook)*

Row 2: With teal, work lps off hook, **do not turn.**

Row 3: Ch 1, skip first vertical bar, sl st in top strand of next horizontal bar, draw up lp in top strand of each horizontal bar across to last horizontal bar, sl st in top strand of last horizontal bar, turn. *(13 lps on hook)*

Row 4: With blue, work lps off hook, **do not turn.**

Row 5: Ch 1, skip first vertical bar, sl st in top strand of next horizontal bar, draw up lp in top strand of each horizontal bar across to last horizontal bar, sl st in top strand of last horizontal bar, turn. *(11 lps on hook)*

Rows 6-14: Repeat rows 2-5 consecutively, ending with row 2 and 3 lps on hook.

Row 15: Ch 1, sl st in top strand of each horizontal bar across. Fasten off.

Easing to fit, sew Base to bottom of Sides, stuffing before closing.

ROUND BLOCK
Top/Bottom Piece (make 2)

Row 1: With yellow, ch 8, draw up lp in second ch from hook, draw up lp in each ch across, turn. *(8 lps on hook)*

Row 2: With lime, work lps off hook, **do not turn.**

Row 3: Ch 1, skip first vertical bar, draw up lp in top strand of each horizontal bar across, turn.

Row 4: With yellow, work lps off hook, **do not turn.**

Row 5: Ch 1, skip first vertical bar, draw up lp in top strand of each horizontal bar across, turn.

Rows 6-84: Repeat rows 2-5 consecutively, ending with row 4.

Row 85: Ch 1, skip first vertical bar, sl st in top strand of each horizontal bar across. Fasten off.

With tapestry needle, weave yellow through ends of rows on one side, pull tight to gather into a circle; secure. Matching sts, sew first and last rows together.

Side

Row 1: With yellow, ch 12, draw up lp in second ch from hook, draw up lp in each ch across, turn. *(12 lps on hook)*

Row 2: With lime, work lps off hook, **do not turn.**

Row 3: Ch 1, skip first vertical bar, draw up lp in top strand of each horizontal bar across, turn.

Row 4: With yellow, work lps off hook, **do not turn.**

Row 5: Ch 1, skip first vertical bar, draw up lp in top strand of each horizontal bar across, turn.

Rows 6-112: Repeat rows 2-5 consecutively, ending with row 4.

Row 113: Ch 1, skip first vertical bar, sl st in top strand of each horizontal bar across. Leaving long end for sewing, fasten off.

Matching sts, sew first and last rows together.

Easing to fit and matching row colors, sew Top and Bottom to Side, stuffing before closing.♦

Dandy Diamonds
continued from page 75

Row 30: Repeat row 6.

Row 31: Ch 1, skip first vertical bar, draw up lp in each vertical bar across, turn.

Row 32: With white, repeat row 6.

Row 33: Ch 1, skip first vertical bar, draw up lp in each vertical bar across, turn.

Rows 34-389: Repeat rows 2-33 consecutively, ending with row 5.

Row 390: With blue, draw through one lp on hook, (yo, draw through 2 lps on hook) across.

Row 391: Ch 1, skip first vertical bar, sl st in each vertical bar across. Fasten off. *(23 sl sts)*

PANEL B (make 2)

Row 1: With white, ch 16, draw up lp in second ch from hook, draw up lp in each ch across, turn. *(16 lps on hook)*

Row 2: With blue, draw through one lp on hook, (yo, draw through 2 lps on hook) 7 times, ch 3, (yo, draw through 2 lps on hook) across, **do not turn.**

Note: Push ch-3 to front of each row throughout.

Row 3: Ch 1, skip first vertical bar, draw up lp in each vertical bar across, turn.

Row 4: With white, repeat row 2.

Row 5: Ch 1, skip first vertical bar, draw up lp in each vertical bar across, turn.

Row 6: With blue, draw through one lp on hook, (yo, draw through 2 lps on hook) 6 times, ch 3, (yo, draw through 2 lps on hook) 2 times, ch 3, (yo, draw through 2 lps on hook) across, **do not turn.**

Row 7: Ch 1, skip first vertical bar, draw up lp in each vertical bar across, turn.

Row 8: With white, repeat row 6.

Row 9: Ch 1, skip first vertical bar, draw up lp in each vertical bar across, turn.

Row 10: With blue, draw through one lp on hook, (yo, draw through 2 lps on hook) 5 times, ch 3, *(yo, draw through 2 lps on hook) 4 times, ch 3, (yo, draw through 2 lps on hook) across, **do not turn.**

Row 11: Ch 1, skip first vertical bar, draw up lp in each vertical bar across, turn.

Row 12: With white, repeat row 10.

Row 13: Ch 1, skip first vertical bar, draw up lp in each vertical bar across, turn.

Row 14: Repeat row 6.

Row 15: Ch 1, skip first vertical bar, draw up lp in each vertical bar across, turn.

Row 16: With white, repeat row 6.

Row 17: Ch 1, skip first vertical bar, draw up lp in each vertical bar across, turn.

Rows 18-389: Repeat rows 2-17 consecutively, ending with row 5.

Row 390: With blue, draw through one lp on hook, (yo, draw through 2 lps on hook) across.

Row 391: Ch 1, skip first vertical bar, sl st in each vertical bar across. Fasten off. *(15 sl sts)*

EDGING

Rnd 1: Working around outer edge of one Panel, with predominantly blue side facing you, using F hook and white, join with sc in first sl st on last row of Panel, ch 1, sc in same st, ch 1, skip next st, (sc in next st, ch 1, skip next st) across to last st, (sc, ch 1, sc) in last st; working in ends of rows, ch 1, skip next white section, (sc in next blue section, ch 1, skip next white section) across; working in starting ch on opposite side of row 1, (sc, ch 1, sc) in first ch, (ch 1, skip next ch, sc in next ch) across to last ch, ch 1, (sc, ch 1, sc) in last ch; working in ends of rows, ch 1, skip next white section, (sc in next blue section, ch 1, skip next white section) across, join with sl st in first sc.

Rnds 2-3: Sl st in next ch sp, ch 1, (sc, ch 1, sc) in same sp, ch 1, (sc in next ch sp, ch 1) around with (sc, ch 1, sc, ch 1) in each corner ch sp, join. At end of last rnd, fasten off.

Repeat Edging around each Panel.

JOINING

Holding one Panel A and one Panel B wrong sides together, matching long edges, with F hook and blue, join with sl st in corner ch sp at bottom of first Panel, ch 1, sl st in corner ch sp at bottom of second Panel, (ch 1, sl st in next ch sp on first Panel, ch 1, sl st in next ch sp on second Panel) across. Fasten off.

Alternating Panel A and Panel B as shown in photo, join remaining Panels in same manner.

BORDER

Rnd 1: Working around entire outer edge of Afghan, with predominantly blue side facing you, with F hook and blue, join with sc in any corner ch sp, ch 1, sc in same sp, ch 1, (sc in next ch sp or in next joining seam, ch 1) across to next corner ch sp, *(sc, ch 1, sc) in next corner ch sp, ch 1, (sc in next ch sp or in next joining seam, ch 1) across to next corner ch sp; repeat from * around, join with sl st in first sc.

Rnd 2: Sl st in next ch sp, ch 1; working from left to right, **reverse sc** *(see Stitch Guide on page 11)* in next ch sp to the right, ch 1, (reverse sc in next ch sp, ch 1) around, join. Fasten off.♦

Lullaby Love

DESIGNED BY MARY ANN SIPES

Sweet angel songs lull baby to sleep when he's snuggled cozy and warm in this heavenly creation that works up like a dream!

SIZE: 31" x 42½".

MATERIALS: Pompadour sport yarn—13 oz. green and 9 oz. white; G double-ended swivel and F hooks or hook size needed to obtain gauge.

GAUGE: With **double-ended hook,** 11 pattern sts *(see row 3)* = 4"; 10 rows = 1".

SPECIAL STITCHES: For **V st,** (dc, ch 1, dc) in next st or ch sp.

For **beginning Vst (beg V st),** ch 4, dc in same st or sp.

NOTES: Read General Instructions on page 6 before beginning pattern.

Use double-ended hook unless otherwise stated.

AFGHAN

Row 1: With green, ch 150, draw up lp in second ch from hook, draw up lp in each ch across, turn. *(150 lps on hook)*

Row 2: With white, work lps off hook, **do not turn.**

Row 3: Ch 1, skip first vertical bar, (yo, draw up lp in next 2 vertical bars at same time) across to last vertical bar *(pattern sts established)*, draw up lp in last vertical bar, turn.

Row 4: With green, work lps off hook, **do not turn.**

Row 5: Ch 1, skip first vertical bar, (yo, draw up lp in next 2 vertical bars at same time) across to last vertical bar, draw up lp in last vertical bar, turn.

Rows 6-384: Repeat rows 2-5 consecutively, ending with row 4.

Row 385: Ch 1, skip first vertical bar, sl st in each vertical bar across. Fasten off.

BORDER

Rnd 1: Working around outer edge, with predominantly white side facing you, using F hook for remainder of pattern, join green with sc in first st of last row, 2 sc in same st, (ch 1, skip next st, sc in next st) across to last st, ch 1, 3 sc in last st, ch 1, evenly space (sc, ch 1) 98 times across ends of rows; working in starting ch on opposite side of row 1, 3 sc in first ch, (ch 1, skip next ch, sc in next ch) across to last ch, ch 1, 3 sc in last ch, ch 1, evenly space (sc, ch 1) 98 times across ends of rows, join with sl st in first sc. Fasten off. *(76 sc and 75 ch sps across each short edge between center corner sc, 101 sc and 99 ch sps across each long edge between center corner sc)*

Rnd 2: Join white with sl st in any center corner st, (ch 4, dc, ch 1, dc) in same st, [◊skip next ch sp, *V st (see Special Stitches) in next ch sp, skip next ch sp; repeat from * across to next corner◊, (dc, ch 1, dc, ch 1, dc) in next corner st]; repeat between [ ] 2 more times; repeat between ◊◊, join with sl st in third ch of ch-4. Fasten off.

Rnd 3: Join green with sl st in first ch sp of any corner, **beg V st** *(see Special Stitches),* ch 1, V st in next ch sp of same corner, *[V st in ch sp of each V st across to next corner], V st in next ch sp, ch 1, V st in next ch sp; repeat from * 2 more times; repeat between [ ], join. Fasten off.

Rnd 4: Join white with sl st in any corner ch sp, (ch 4, dc, ch 1, dc) in same sp, V st in each V st around with (dc, ch 1, dc, ch 1, dc) in each corner ch sp, join. Fasten off.

Rnd 5: Repeat rnd 3.

Rnd 6: (Sl st, ch 1, sc) in first ch sp, ch 3, hdc in third ch from hook, (sc in next ch sp or V st, ch 3, hdc in third ch from hook) around, join with sl st in first sc. Fasten off.♦

Parfait Pal

DESIGNED BY MARY ANN SIPES

Yummy stripes of ice cream colors worked in a simple one-piece pattern make this delicious design a treat to crochet!

SIZE: 34" x 44½".

MATERIALS: Pompadour sport yarn—8 oz. white, 3 oz. each blue, yellow, green and pink; G double-ended swivel and F hooks or hook size needed to obtain gauge.

GAUGES: With **double-ended hook,** 5 cr sts = 2"; 12 rows = 2".

SPECIAL STITCHES: For **dc lp,** yo, draw up lp in next vertical bar, yo, draw through 2 lps on hook.

For **cross stitch (cr st),** skip next vertical bar, dc lp in next vertical bar; working in front of st just made, dc lp in skipped vertical bar.

For **beginning dc cross st (beg dc cr st),** sl st in next st, ch 3; working in front of ch-3 just made, dc in first st.

for **dc cross stitch (dc cr st),** skip next st, dc in next st; working in front of dc just made, dc in skipped st.

NOTES: Read General Instructions on page 6 before beginning pattern.

Use double-ended hook unless otherwise stated.

AFGHAN

Row 1: With white, ch 208, draw up lp in second ch from hook, draw up lp in each ch across, turn. *(208 lps on hook)*

Row 2: With blue, work lps off hook, **do not turn.**

Row 3: Ch 1, skip first vertical bar, **cr st** *(see Special Stitches)* across to last vertical bar, **dc lp** *(see Special Stitches)* in last vertical bar, turn.

Row 4: With white, work lps off hook, **do not turn.**

Row 5: Ch 1, skip first vertical bar, draw up lp in each vertical bar across, turn.

Row 6: With yellow, work lps off hook, **do not turn.**

Row 7: Ch 1, skip first vertical bar, cr st across to last vertical bar, dc lp in last vertical bar, turn.

Rows 8-180: Working in color sequence of white, green, white, pink, white, blue, white and yellow, repeat rows 4-7 consecutively, ending with row 4 and white.

Row 181: Ch 1, sl st in each vertical bar across, turn, **do not fasten off.**

BORDER

Rnd 1: Working around outer edge, using F hook for remainder of pattern, ch 3 *(counts as first dc),* (dc, ch 1, 2 dc) in first st, ch 1, skip next 2 sts, (2 dc in next st, ch 1, skip next 2 sts) across to last st, (2 dc, ch 1, 2 dc) in last st; working in ends of rows, ch 1, (2 dc in next cr st row, ch 1) across; working in starting ch on opposite side of row 1, (2 dc, ch 1, 2 dc) in first ch, ch 1, skip next 2 chs, (2 dc in next ch, ch 1, skip next 2 chs) across to last ch, (2 dc, ch 1, 2 dc) in last ch; working in ends of rows, ch 1, (2 dc in next cr st row, ch 1) across, join with sl st in top of ch-3. *(70 2-dc groups across each long edge between corner ch-1 sps, 47 2-dc groups across each short edge between corner ch-1 sps)*

Rnd 2: Beg dc cr st *(see Special Stitches),* ch 1, (2 dc, ch 1, 2 dc) in next corner ch sp, ch 1; **dc cr st** *(see Special Stitches),* *(ch 1, skip next ch sp, dc cr st) across to next corner ch sp, ch 1, (2 dc, ch 1, 2 dc) in next corner ch sp, ch 1, dc cr st; repeat from * 2 more times, ch 1, skip next ch sp, (dc cr st, ch 1, skip next ch sp) across, join with sl st in top of beg dc cr st.

Rnd 3: Beg dc cr st, ch 1, skip next ch sp, dc cr st, ch 1, (2 dc, ch 1, 2 dc) in next corner ch sp, ch 1, *dc cr st, (ch 1, skip next ch sp, dc cr st) across to next corner ch sp, ch 1, (2 dc, ch 1, 2 dc) in next corner ch sp, ch 1; repeat from * 2 more times, (dc cr st, ch 1, skip next ch sp) across, join.

Rnd 4: Ch 1, sc in each st and in each ch sp around, join with sl st in first sc. Fasten off.♦

Household
Hurrahs

Chapter Three

Aspen Twilight Afghan

DESIGNED BY DARLA FANTON

Peaks of soothing twilight colors gently paint the canvas of this cozy fireside warmer that works up quickly in worsted yarn and a large-size hook.

FINISHED SIZE: 44" x 71".

MATERIALS: Worsted yarn—22 oz. blue, 20 oz. variegated and 18 oz. brown; tapestry needle; K double-ended and K crochet hooks or hook sizes needed to obtain gauges.

GAUGES: With **K double-ended hook,** 7 clusters = 3"; 7 rows = 1". With **K crochet hook,** 10 sts = 4".

NOTE: Read General Instructions on page 6 before beginning pattern.

AFGHAN

Row 1: With blue, ch 194, pull up lp in second ch from hook, pull up lp in each ch across, turn. *(194 lps on hook)*

Row 2: To **work lps off hook,** with variegated, pull through first lp on hook, (ch 1, yo, pull through 3 lps on hook—*cluster made)* across to last 2 lps on hook, ch 1, yo, pull through last 2 lps on hook, **do not turn.**

Row 3: Ch 1, skip first vertical bar, pull up lp in both vertical bars of next cl at same time, (yo, pull up lp in both vertical bars of next cl at same time) across to last vertical bar, yo, pull up lp in last vertical bar, turn.

Row 4: With brown, repeat row 2.

Row 5: Repeat row 3.

Row 6: With blue, repeat row 2.

Row 7: Ch 1, pull up lp in first vertical bar and first vertical bar of next cl at same time, (yo, pull up lp in second vertical bar of same cl and first vertical bar of next cl at same time) across to last 2 vertical bars, yo, pull up lp in second vertical bar of same cl and last vertical bar at same time, turn.

Rows 8-480: Repeat rows 2-7 consecutively, ending with row 6.

Row 481: Ch 1, sc in first vertical bar and first vertical bar of next cl at same time, (sc in second vertical bar of same cl and first vertical bar of next cl at same time) across to last 2 vertical bars, sc in second vertical bar of same cl and last vertical bar at same time, **do not turn.**

For **first side edging,** with K crochet hook, working in ends of rows, evenly space 159 sc across, sl st in first ch on opposite side of row 1. Fasten off.

For **second side edging,** with K crochet hook and blue, working in ends of rows on opposite side, join with sc in first row, evenly space 158 more sc across, sl st in first st on last row, **do not fasten off.**

BORDER

Rnd 1: Working around outer edge, ch 2 *(counts as first hdc),* 2 hdc in same st, hdc in each st across to next corner st, 3 hdc in next corner st; working in sts across first side edging, hdc in each st across to next corner; working in starting ch on opposite side of row 1, 3 hdc in first ch, (hdc in next ch, skip next ch) across to last ch, 3 hdc in last ch; working in sts across second side edging, hdc in each st across, join with sl st in top of ch-2. Fasten off. *(98 hdc across each short end between center corner sts, 161 hdc across each long edge between center corner sts)*

Rnd 2: Join variegated with sl st in first center corner st, ch 2, 2 hdc in same st, [*ch 1, skip next st, (hdc, ch 1, hdc) in next st*; repeat between ** across to 2 sts before next center corner st, ch 1, skip next 2 sts, 3 hdc in next corner st; repeat between ** across to one st before next center corner st, ch 1, skip next st], 3 hdc in next st; repeat between [ ], join. Fasten off.

Rnd 3: Join blue with sc in first center corner st, 2 sc in same st, *[sc in next st; working over next ch sp, hdc in next skipped st on rnd before last, (skip next hdc, sc in next ch sp, skip next hdc; working over next ch sp, hdc in next skipped st on rnd before last) across to next 3-hdc corner, sc in next st], 3 sc in next st; repeat from * 2 more times; repeat between [ ], join with sl st in first sc. Fasten off.♦

Scraps & Suds

DESIGNED BY DARLA FANTON

Stitch this festive pot holder and dishcloth set in any cheerful color combination of sport weight cotton yarn, and you'll feel like whistling while you work!

Dishcloth

FINISHED SIZE: 8" x 9".

MATERIALS: 100 percent cotton sport yarn—18 yds. each white and purple, 9 yds. rose and 5 yds. aqua; J double-ended and I crochet hooks or hook sizes needed to obtain gauges.

GAUGES: With **double-ended hook,** 4 clusters and 3 vertical bars worked in pattern established in row 2 = 3"; 10 rows = 2". With **I hook,** 3 sts = 1".

NOTE: Read General Instructions on page 6 before beginning pattern.

SPECIAL STITCH: For **cluster (cl),** yo, pull through 4 lps on hook.

DISHCLOTH

Row 1: With double-ended hook and purple, ch 37, yo, pull up lp in third ch from hook, (yo, skip next ch, pull up lp in next ch) across, turn. *(37 lps on hook)*

Row 2: To **work lps off hook,** with white, pull through first lp on hook, ch 1, **cl** *(see Special Stitch),* ch 1, yo, pull through 2 lps on hook, (ch 1, cl, ch 1, yo, pull through 2 lps on hook) across, **do not turn.**

Row 3: Ch 1, skip first vertical bar, (yo, pull up lp in top of next cl, yo, pull up lp in next vertical bar) across, turn.

Rows 4-32: Working in color sequence of rose, white, aqua, white, rose, white, purple and white, repeat rows 2 and 3 alternately, ending with row 2 and purple.

Row 33: Ch 1, sc in first vertical bar, sc in each ch, in top of each cl and in each vertical bar across, **do not turn or fasten off.** *Change to I hook for remainder of pattern.*

Row 34: For **first side edging,** working in ends of rows, evenly spacing sts so piece lays flat, sc across to next corner. Fasten off.

Row 35: For **second side edging,** working in ends of rows on opposite side, join purple with sc in first row, evenly spacing sts so piece lays flat, sc across to next corner, sl st in first sc of row 33, **do not fasten off.**

Rnd 36: For **border,** working in rnds, ch 2 *(counts as first hdc),* 2 hdc in same st, skip next st, (hdc in next st, skip next st) across to last st on this side, 3 hdc in last st, hdc in each st across to next corner; working in starting ch on opposite side of row 1, 3 hdc in first ch, skip next ch, (hdc in next ch, skip next ch) across to last ch on this side, 3 hdc in last ch, hdc in each st across, join with sl st in top of ch-2. Fasten off.

Pot Holder

SIZE: 7¼" square without hanging loop.

MATERIALS FOR TWO: 100 percent cotton sport yarn—64 yds. white, 54 yds. purple, 24 yds. rose and 20 yds. aqua; I double-ended and I crochet hooks or hook sizes needed to obtain gauges.

GAUGES: With **double-ended hook,** 5 clusters and 4 vertical bars worked in pattern established in row 2 = 3"; 9 rows = 1". With **I hook,** 3 sts = 1".

NOTE: Read General Instructions on page 6 before beginning pattern.

SPECIAL STITCH: For **cluster (cl),** yo, pull through 4 lps on hook.

POT HOLDER (make 2)

Row 1: With double-ended hook and purple, ch 37, pull up lp in second ch from hook, pull up lp in each ch across, turn. *(37 lps on hook)*

Row 2: To **work lps off hook,** with white, pull through first lp on hook, ch 1, **cl** *(see Special Stitch),* ch 1, yo, pull through 2 lps on hook, (ch 1, cl, ch 1, yo, pull through 2 lps on hook) across, **do not turn.**

Row 3: Ch 1, skip first vertical bar, (pull up lp in sp before next cl, pull up lp under all 3 bars

continued on page 91

Sachets in a Snap

DESIGNED BY LORI ZELLER

Small amounts of cotton thread are all it takes to quickly stitch these sweet little sachets that make the perfect last-minute gift for a bridal shower or housewarming!

FINISHED SIZE: 2½" square.
MATERIALS FOR BOTH: Size 10 crochet cotton—30 yds. blue, 25 yds. pink and 20 yds. pink variegated; potpourri; used fabric softener dryer sheet; craft glue or hot glue gun; tapestry needle; G double-ended and B hooks or hook sizes needed to obtain gauge.

GAUGE: With **double-ended hook,** 3 sc lps worked in pattern = 1"; 8 rows = 1".

SPECIAL STITCH: For **single crochet loop (sc lp),** pull up lp in specified ch or bar, ch 1.

NOTE: Read General Instructions on page 6 before beginning pattern.

POTPOURRI POUCH (make 2)

Cut one 2¼" x 4½" piece of dryer sheet. Fold in half crosswise; glue two sides together. Stuff with potpourri and glue opening closed.

SACHET SIDE (make 4)

Row 1: With double-ended hook and one strand each pink and variegated held together, ch 12, yo, **sc lp** *(see Special Stitch)* in second ch from hook, (yo, skip next ch, sc lp in next ch) across, turn. *(13 lps on hook)*

Row 2: With two strands blue held together, work lps off hook, **do not turn.**

Row 3: Skip first vertical bar, pull up lp in each vertical bar across, turn.

Row 4: With one strand each pink and variegated held together, work lps off hook, **do not turn.**

Row 5: Ch 1, skip first vertical bar, (yo, pull up lp in next 2 vertical bars at same time, yo, pull through one lp on hook) across, turn.

Rows 6-20: Repeat rows 2-5 consecutively, ending with row 4. At end of last row, fasten off.

For **first Sachet edging,** holding two Sides with predominantly blue side facing, working through both thicknesses, using B hook and one strand pink, join with sc in first st of last row, ch 3, sc in same st, ch 3, (sc in top strand of next **horizontal bar**—*see illustration,* ch 3) across to last horizontal bar, (sc, ch 3, sc) in last horizontal bar; working in ends of rows, ch 3, evenly space (sc in next row, ch 3) across 12 times; working in starting ch on opposite side of row 1, (sc, ch 3, sc) in first ch, ch 3, (sc in next ch, ch 3) across to last ch, (sc, ch 3, sc) in last ch, insert one Potpourri Pouch; working in ends of rows, ch 3, evenly space (sc in next row, ch 3) across 12 times, join with sl st in first sc. Fasten off.

For **second Sachet edging,** holding remaining two Sides with predominantly pink side facing outward, using one strand blue, work same as first Sachet edging.♦

Horizontal Bar

Scraps & Suds

continued from page 89

of next cl at same time, pull up lp in sp after same cl, pull up lp in next vertical bar) across, turn.

Rows 4-5: With rose, repeat rows 2 and 3.

Rows 6-7: Repeat rows 2 and 3.

Rows 8-9: With aqua, repeat rows 2 and 3.

Rows 10-11: Repeat rows 2 and 3.

Rows 12-13: With rose, repeat rows 2 and 3.

Rows 14-15: Repeat rows 2 and 3.

Rows 16-17: With purple, repeat rows 2 and 3.

Rows 18-19: Repeat rows 2 and 3.

Rows 20-21: With purple, repeat rows 2 and 3.

Rows 22-23: Repeat rows 2 and 3.

Rows 24-25: With aqua, repeat rows 2 and 3.

Rows 26-27: Repeat rows 2 and 3.

Rows 28-29: With rose, repeat rows 2 and 3.

Rows 30-31: Repeat rows 2 and 3.

Rows 32-33: With aqua, repeat rows 2 and 3.

Rows 34-35: Repeat rows 2 and 3.

Rows 36-37: With purple, repeat rows 2 and 3.

Rows 38-39: Repeat rows 2 and 3.

Rows 40-41: With purple, repeat rows 2 and 3.

Rows 42-43: Repeat rows 2 and 3.

Rows 44-56: Repeat rows 4-16.

Row 57: Ch 1, sc in first vertical bar, (sc under all 3 bars of next cl at once, sc in next vertical bar) across, **do not turn or fasten off.** *Change to I hook for remainder of pattern.*

Row 58: For **first side edging,** working in ends of rows, evenly spacing sts so piece lays flat, sc across to next corner. Fasten off.

Row 59: For **second side edging,** working in ends of rows on opposite side, join purple with sc in first row, evenly spacing sts so piece lays flat, sc across to next corner, sl st in first sc of row 57. **Do not fasten off.**

Rnd 60: For **border,** working in rnds, ch 2 *(counts as first hdc),* 2 hdc in same st, hdc in each st across to last st on this side, sl st in last st; for **hanging loop,** ch 9, sl st in first ch to form ring, sc in ring, (ch 1, sc in ring) 8 times, sl st in same st as last sl st, hdc in each st across to next corner; working in starting ch on opposite side of row 1, 3 hdc in first ch, skip next ch, (hdc in next ch, skip next ch) across to last ch, 3 hdc in last ch, hdc in each st across, join with sl st in top of ch-2. Fasten off.♦

Independence Day

DESIGNED BY ANNE HALLIDAY

Proudly display Old Glory's colors with this distinctively patriotic afghan that's worked in easy-to-make blocks for a great take-along project.

FINISHED SIZE: 50¾" x 63¼".

MATERIALS: Worsted yarn—35 oz. tan, 9 oz. each burgundy and blue; tapestry needle; I double-ended, H and I hooks or hook sizes needed to obtain gauges.

GAUGES: With **double-ended hook,** 11 sts = 3"; 8 rows = 1". With **I hook,** 7 sc = 2". With **H hook,** 10 sts = 3". Each Block is 6¼" square.

NOTE: Read General Instructions on page 6 before beginning pattern.

BLOCK A (make 32)

Row 1: With double-ended hook and tan, ch 11, pull up lp in second ch from hook, pull up lp in each ch across, turn. *(11 lps on hook)*

Row 2: With burgundy, work lps off hook, **do not turn.**

Row 3: Ch 1, skip first vertical bar, pull up lp in each vertical bar across, turn. *Predominantly burgundy side is right side of Block.*

Row 4: With tan, work lps off hook, **do not turn.**

Row 5: Ch 1, skip first vertical bar, pull up lp in each vertical bar across, turn.

Rows 6-22: Repeat rows 2-5 consecutively, ending with row 2.

Row 23: Ch 1, skip first vertical bar, sl st in each vertical bar across. Fasten off.

Rnd 24: Working in rnds, with predominantly burgundy side facing you, with I hook and tan, join with sl st in first sl st of last row, sl st in next 10 sts, ch 1, evenly space 11 sl sts across ends of rows, ch 1; working in starting ch on opposite side of row 1, sl st in next 11 chs, ch 1, evenly space 11 sl sts across ends of rows, ch 1, join with sl st in first sl st. *(11 sl sts across each side between corner chs)*

Rnd 25: Working this rnd in **back lps** only *(see Stitch Guide on page 11),* ch 1, sc in first st, (sc next 2 sts tog, sc in next 3 sts) 2 times, ch 1, dc in next corner ch, ch 1, *sc in next st, (sc next 2 sts tog, sc in next 3 sts) 2 times, ch 1, dc in next corner ch, ch 1; repeat from * around, join with sl st in first sc, **turn.** *(9 sc and 2 ch sps across each side between corner dc)* Drop tan.

Rnd 26: With wrong side facing you, join blue with sc in ch sp before any corner dc, ch 3, skip next dc, (sc in next ch sp or st, ch 3, skip next st) 5 times, *sc in next ch sp, ch 3, skip next dc, (sc in next ch sp or st, ch 3, skip next st) 5 times; repeat from * around, join, **turn.** Fasten off. *(5 ch sps across each side between corner ch sps)*

Rnd 27: With right side facing you; working behind ch sps of last rnd, pick up tan from rnd before last, ch 3 *(counts as first dc),* sc in next st on last rnd, (dc in next skipped st on rnd before last, sc in next st on last rnd) 4 times, (dc, ch 3, dc) in next skipped dc on rnd before last, sc in next st on last rnd, *(dc in next skipped st on rnd before last, sc in next st on last rnd) 5 times, (dc, ch 3, dc) in next skipped dc on rnd before last, sc in next st on last rnd; repeat from * around, join with sl st in top of ch-3, **turn.** *(13 sts across each side between corner ch sps)* Drop tan.

Rnd 28: With wrong side facing you, join burgundy with sc in first ch of any corner ch sp, ch 3, skip next ch, sc in next ch, ch 1, skip next st, (sc in next st, ch 1, skip next st) 6 times, *sc in first ch of next corner ch sp, ch 3, skip next ch, sc in next ch, ch 1, skip next st, (sc in next st, ch 1, skip next st) 6 times; repeat from * around, join with sl st in first sc, **turn.**

Rnd 29: With right side facing you; working behind ch sps of last rnd, pick up tan from rnd before last, ch 3, sc in next st on last rnd, (dc in next skipped st on rnd before last, sc in next st on last rnd) 5 times, (dc, ch 3, dc) in center of next ch sp on rnd before last, sc in next st on last rnd, *(dc in next st on rnd before last, sc in next st on last rnd) 7 times, (dc, ch 3, dc) in center of

continued on page 96

Travel-gan

DESIGNED BY DEBBIE TABOR

For busy sports fans on the go, here's a cozy blanket to chase away the chill at cold-weather games! It's easily portable with its own carrying strap.

FINISHED SIZE: Afghan is 29" x 44".

MATERIALS: Worsted yarn—17 oz. taupe and 12 oz. aran; two 1" strap buckles; tapestry needle; G double-ended and K swivel double-ended hooks or hook sizes needed to obtain gauges.

GAUGES: With **G double-ended hook,** 5 sts = 1"; 8 rows = 1". With **K swivel double-ended hook,** 7 sts = 2"; rows 1-4 = 1".

SPECIAL STITCH: For **double crochet loop (dc lp),** yo, pull up lp in specified bar or st, yo, pull through 2 lps on hook.

NOTE: Read General Instructions on page 6 before beginning pattern.

AFGHAN

Row 1: With K double-ended hook and taupe, ch 100, pull up lp in second ch from hook, pull up lp in each ch across, turn. *(100 lps on hook)*

Row 2: With aran, work lps off hook, **do not turn.**

Row 3: Ch 1, skip first vertical bar, **dc lp** *(see Special Stitch)* in top strand of each **horizontal bar** across *(see illustration)*, turn.

Horizontal Bar

Row 4: With taupe, work lps off hook, **do not turn.**

Row 5: Ch 1, skip first vertical bar, pull up lp in top strand of each hori-zontal bar across, turn.

Rows 6-176: Repeat rows 2-5 consecutively, ending with row 4.

Row 177: Ch 1, skip first vertical bar, sl st in top strand of each horizontal bar across. Fasten off.

For **first side edging,** working in ends of rows across one long edge of Afghan, with K double-ended hook and taupe, join with sc in first row, evenly spacing sts so piece lays flat, sc across to next corner. Fasten off.

For **second side edging,** joining in last row, work same as first side edging on opposite edge.

STRAP (make 2)

Row 1: With G double-ended hook and taupe, ch 7, pull up lp in second ch from hook, pull up lp in each ch across, turn. *(7 lps on hook)*

Row 2: With aran, work lps off hook, **do not turn.**

Row 3: Ch 1, skip first vertical bar, pull up lp under each horizontal bar across, turn.

Row 4: With taupe, work lps off hook, **do not turn.**

Row 5: Ch 1, skip first vertical bar, pull up lp under each horizontal bar across, turn.

Rows 6-120: Repeat rows 2-5 consecutively, ending with row 4.

Row 121: Ch 1, skip first vertical bar, sl st under each horizontal bar across. Fasten off.

HANDLE

Rows 1-68: Repeat same rows of Strap.

Row 69: Repeat row 121 of Strap.

Sew one end of Handle to center of each Strap on one side, forming an "H" shape. Sew buckles to Strap ends.

Fold Afghan in half lengthwise. Roll up, starting at one short end. Buckle Straps around rolled-up Afghan.♦

Independence Day

continued from page 93

next ch sp on rnd before last, sc in next st on last rnd; repeat from * 2 more times, dc in next skipped st on rnd before last, sc in last st on last rnd, join, **do not turn.** Fasten off. *(17 sts across each side between corner ch sps)*

BLOCK B (make 31)

Work same as Block A reversing burgundy and blue. *Predominantly blue side is right side of Block.*

Sew together in seven rows of nine Blocks each, alternating Blocks and keeping row 1 facing same direction.

BORDER

Rnd 1: Working around entire outer edge of Blocks, with H hook and tan, join with sl st in any corner ch sp, (ch 3, dc, ch 3, 2 dc) in same sp, *[dc in next 17 sts, (dc in next ch sp, tr in next seam, dc in next ch sp, dc in next 17 sts) across to next corner ch sp], (2 dc, ch 3, 2 dc) in next corner ch sp; repeat from * 2 more times; repeat between [ ], join with sl st in top of ch-3, **turn.** Fasten off. *(141 sts across each short end between corner ch sps, 181 sts across each long edge between corner ch sps)* Use H hook for remainder of pattern.

Rnd 2: With wrong side facing you, join blue with sc in first ch of any corner ch sp, *[ch 3, skip next ch, sc in next ch, ch 1, skip next st, (sc in next st, ch 1, skip next st) across] to next corner ch sp, sc in first ch of next corner ch sp; repeat from * 2 more times; repeat between [ ], join with sl st in first sc, **turn.** Fasten off.

Rnd 3: With right side facing you; working behind ch sps, join tan with sc in first st after any corner ch sp, *◊(dc in next skipped st on rnd before last, sc in next st on last rnd) across to next corner ch sp, (dc, ch 3, dc) in center of next ch sp on rnd before last◊, sc in next st on last rnd; repeat from * 2 more times; repeat between ◊◊, join with sl st in first sc, **turn.** Fasten off.

Rnd 4: With burgundy, repeat rnd 2.

Rnd 5: Repeat rnd 3.

Rnd 6: Repeat rnd 2.

Rnd 7: Repeat rnd 3, **do not turn or fasten off.**

Rnd 8: Ch 1, sc in first st, ch 1, skip next st, *(sc in next st, ch 1, skip next st) across to next corner ch sp, (sc, ch 2, sc) in next ch sp, ch 1, skip next st; repeat from * around, join.

Rnd 9: (Sl st in next ch sp, ch 1) around with (sl st, ch 2, sl st) in each corner ch sp, join with sl st in first sl st. Fasten off.♦

Floor Protectors

DESIGNED BY SUE PENROD

Protect your floors from nasty scuff marks with these easy-to-stitch little "shoes" made just for chairs!

FINISHED SIZE: 3¼" tall.

MATERIALS FOR FOUR: Worsted yarn—1½ oz. each aran and brown; tapestry needle; G double-ended hook or hook size needed to obtain gauge.

GAUGE: 4 sts = 1"; 7 rows = 1".

NOTE: Read General Instructions on page 6 before beginning pattern.

FLOOR PROTECTOR (make 4)

Row 1: With brown, ch 12, pull up lp in second ch from hook, pull up lp in each ch across, turn. *(12 lps on hook)*

Row 2: With aran, work lps off hook, **do not turn.**

Row 3: Skip first vertical bar, pull up lp under each **horizontal bar** across *(see illustration),* turn.

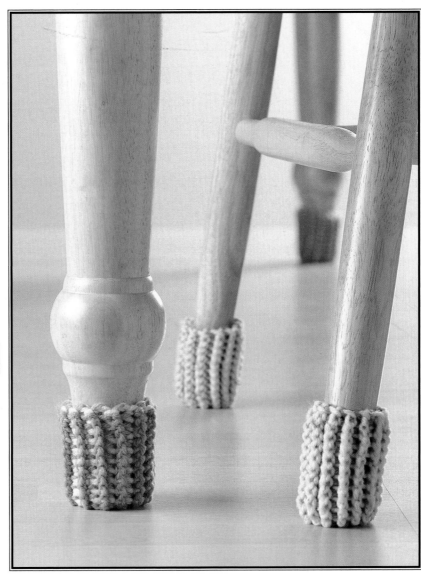

Row 4: With brown, work lps off hook, **do not turn.**

Row 5: Skip first vertical bar, pull up lp under each horizontal bar across, turn.

Rows 6-52 or until piece is long enough to fit around chair leg: Repeat rows 2-5 consecu-

tively, ending with row 4.

Row 53: Skip first vertical bar, sl st under each horizontal bar across; **do not turn; to gather bottom,** leaving lps on hook, pull up lp in end of every other row, yo, pull through all lps on hook, ch 1. Leaving long end for sewing, fasten off.

Sew first and last rows together.♦

Tank Toppers

Designed by Sue Penrod

Use complimentary colors of worsted yarn to stitch this set of pretty tissue covers to accent your bathroom décor!

FINISHED SIZE: Tissue Cover fits boutique-style tissue box. Toilet Paper Cover fits standard toilet tissue roll.

MATERIALS: Worsted yarn—4 oz. each white and blue; three nautical ⅝" shank buttons; one 1" white shank button; tapestry needle; G double-ended hook or hook size needed to obtain gauge.

GAUGE: 4 sts = 1"; 9 rows = 1".

NOTE: Read General Instructions on page 6 before beginning pattern.

TISSUE COVER
Side A (make 2)

Row 1: With blue, ch 20, pull up lp in second ch from hook, pull up lp in each ch across, turn. *(20 lps on hook)*

Row 2: With white, work lps off hook, **do not turn.**

Row 3: Ch 1, skip first vertical bar, pull up lp in each vertical bar across, turn.

Row 4: With blue, work lps off hook, **do not turn.**

Row 5: Ch 1, skip first vertical bar, pull up lp in each vertical bar across, turn.

Rows 6-44: Repeat rows 2-5 consecutively, ending with row 4.

Row 45: Ch 1, skip first vertical bar, sl st in each vertical bar across. Fasten off.

Side B (make one as written, make one reversing colors)

Rows 1-44: Repeat same rows of Side A.

Row 45: Ch 1, skip first vertical bar, pull up lp in each vertical bar across, turn.

Row 46: With white, work lps off hook, **do not turn.**

Row 47: Ch 1, skip first vertical bar, pull up lp in each vertical bar across, turn.

Row 48: For **top,** with blue, pull through first lp on hook, (yo, pull through 2 lps on hook) across to last 3 lps on hook; for **decrease,** yo, pull through last 3 lps on hook, **do not turn.**

Row 49: Ch 1, skip first vertical bar, pull up lp in each vertical bar across, turn. *(18 lps on hook)*

Row 50: With white, work lps off hook, **do not turn.**

Row 51: Ch 1, skip first vertical bar, pull up lp in each vertical bar across, turn.

Rows 52-80: Repeat rows 48-51 consecutively, ending with row 48 and *2 vertical bars* in last row.

Row 81: Ch 1, skip first vertical bar, sl st in last vertical bar. Fasten off.

Sew Sides A and B together as shown in diagram. Sew unsewn edges of Sides A on each end together. Sew top of each Side A to ends of rows on straight edge of each Side B. Tack inside corners on angled edge of each Side B together leaving 3¼" unsewn for tissue opening.

Sew three small buttons evenly spaced to one angled edge.

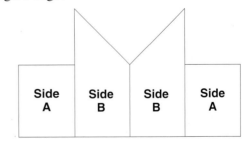

TOILET TISSUE COVER
Top

Row 1: With blue, ch 7, pull up lp in second ch from hook, pull up lp in each ch across, turn. *(7 lps on hook)*

Row 2: With white, work lps off hook, **do not turn.**

Row 3: Ch 1, skip first vertical bar, pull up lp

continued on page 101

Colorful Coasters

DESIGNED BY SUE PENROD

Entertain in festive style or brighten your kitchen décor with a set of cheery coasters stitched in a rainbow of colors!

FINISHED SIZE: 4½" across.
MATERIALS FOR ONE: Worsted yarn—scraps of two contrasting colors; tapestry needle; G double-ended hook or hook size needed to obtain gauge.
GAUGE: 4 sts = 1"; 7 rows = 1".
NOTE: Read General Instructions on page 6 before beginning pattern.

COASTER

Row 1: With first color, ch 8, pull up lp in second ch from hook, pull up lp in each ch across, turn. *(8 lps on hook)*

Row 2: With second color, work lps off hook, **do not turn.**

Row 3: Skip first vertical bar, pull up lp under each **horizontal bar** across *(see illustration)*, turn.

Horizontal Bar

Row 4: With first color, work lps off hook, **do not turn.**

Row 5: Skip first vertical bar, pull up lp under each horizontal bar across, turn.

Rows 6-120: Repeat rows 2-5 consecutively, ending with row 4.

Row 121: Skip first vertical bar, sl st under each horizontal bar across, **do not turn;** leaving lps on hook, pull up lp in end of every other row across, yo, pull through all lps on hook, ch 1. Leaving long end for sewing, fasten off.

Sew first and last rows together.♦

Tank Toppers

continued from page 99

under each **horizontal bar** *(see illustration above)* across, turn.

Row 4: With blue, work lps off hook, **do not turn.**

Row 5: Ch 1, skip first vertical bar, pull up lp under each horizontal bar across, turn.

Rows 6-116: Repeat rows 2-5 consecutively, ending with row 4.

Row 117: Ch 1, skip first vertical bar, sl st under each horizontal bar across, **do not turn;** to **gather center of Top,** ch 1, pull up lp in end of every other row across, yo, pull through all lps on hook, ch 1. Leaving long end for sewing, fasten off. Sew first and last rows together.

Side

Row 1: With blue, ch 18, pull up lp in second ch from hook, pull up lp in each ch across, turn. *(18 lps on hook)*

Row 2: With white, work lps off hook, **do not turn.**

Row 3: Ch 1, skip first vertical bar, pull up lp in each vertical bar across, turn.

Row 4: With blue, work lps off hook, **do not turn.**

Row 5: Ch 1, skip first vertical bar, pull up lp in each vertical bar across, turn.

Rows 6-116: Repeat rows 2-5 consecutively, ending with row 4.

Row 117: Ch 1, skip first vertical bar, sl st in each vertical bar across. Leaving long end for sewing, fasten off. Sew first and last rows together.

Sew Top to Side. Sew large button to center of Top.♦

Striped Delight Pillow

DESIGNED BY DEBBIE TABOR

Simple techniques and stylish design combine to create a sensational pillow with decorative flair!

FINISHED SIZE: 16" square.

MATERIALS: Worsted yarn—2½ oz. each white and black; one black 1⅛" button; one white 1⅛" button; 14" pillow form; tapestry needle; J double-ended hook or hook size needed to obtain gauge.

GAUGE: 4 sts = 1"; 7 rows = 1".

NOTE: Read General Instructions on page 6 before beginning pattern.

SIDE A
Quarter Panel (make 4)

Row 1: With white, ch 4, pull up lp in second ch from hook, yo 2 times, pull up lp in next ch, pull up lp in last ch, turn. *(6 lps on hook)*

Row 2: With black, work lps off hook, **do not turn.**

Row 3: Ch 1, skip first vertical bar, pull up lp in top strand of next 2 **horizontal bars** *(see illustration)*, yo 2 times, pull up lp in top strand of last 3 horizontal bars, turn. *(8 lps on hook)*

Horizontal Bar

Row 4: With white, work lps off hook, **do not turn.**

Row 5: Ch 1, skip first vertical bar, pull up lp in top strand of next 3 horizontal bars, yo 2 times, pull up lp in top strand of last 4 horizontal bars, turn. *(10 lps on hook)*

Row 6: With black, work lps off hook, **do not turn.**

Row 7: Ch 1, skip first vertical bar, pull up lp in top strand of each horizontal bar across to center horizontal bar, yo 2 times, pull up lp in top strand of center horizontal bar and each horizontal bar across, turn. *(12 lps on hook)*

Row 8: With white, work lps off hook, **do not turn.**

Row 9: Repeat row 7.

Rows 10-48: Repeat rows 6-9 consecutively, ending with row 8 and *52 lps on hook* in last row.

Row 49: Ch 1, skip first vertical bar, sl st in top strand of each horizontal bar across. Fasten off.

continued on page 105

Teal Treasure Afghan

DESIGNED BY CAROLYN CHRISTMAS

Wrap yourself in cozy comfort with the warm texture and rich color of this simple but elegant afghan creation.

FINISHED SIZE: 42" square.

MATERIALS: Worsted yarn—11 oz. each dk. teal and med. teal; K crochet hook; Crochenit™ hook or hook size needed to obtain gauge.

GAUGE: With **Crochenit™ hook,** 1 shell = 1"; 6 rows = 1½".

SPECIAL STITCH: For **dc group,** 3 dc in ch sp or in end of row.

CROCHENIT™ STITCH: Shell Stitch #300

NOTE: Read General Instructions and Crochenit™ Tips on page 8 before beginning pattern.

AFGHAN

Row 1: With Crochenit™ hook and dk. teal, ch 112, pull up lp in second ch from hook, pull up lp in each ch across, turn. *(112 lps on hook)*

Row 2: To **work lps off hook,** with med. teal, pull through one lp on hook, *ch 2, yo, pull through 4 lps on hook *(counts as ch-3 and shell);* repeat from * across, **do not turn.**

Row 3: Ch 1, skipping shells, pull up lp in each ch across, turn. *(112 lps on hook)*

Row 4: Repeat row 2.

Row 5: Ch 1, skipping shells, pull up lp in each ch across, turn.

Rows 6-152: Repeat rows 2-5 consecutively, ending with row 4. At end of last row, fasten off both colors.

BORDER

Rnd 1: Working around outer edge, with K hook and dk. teal, join with sl st in first ch sp of last row, (ch 3, 2 dc, ch 2, 3 dc) in same sp *(corner made),* work **dc group** *(see Special Stitch)* in each ch sp across to last ch sp, (3 dc, ch 2, 3 dc) in last ch sp; evenly space 35 dc groups across ends of rows; working in sps between shells on opposite side of row 1, (3 dc, ch 2, 3 dc) in first sp, work dc group in each sp across to last sp, (3 dc, ch 2, 3 dc) in last sp; evenly space 35 dc groups across ends of rows, join with sl st in top of ch-3. Fasten off.

Rnd 2: Join med. teal with sc in first corner ch sp, ch 2, sc in same sp, ch 3, (sc in center st of next dc group, ch 3) across to next corner ch sp, *(sc, ch 2, sc) in next corner ch sp, ch 3, (sc in center st of next dc group, ch 3) across to next corner ch sp; repeat from * around, join with sl st in first sc. Fasten off.

Rnd 3: Join dk. teal with sc in first corner ch sp, (2 dc, ch 2, 2 dc) in next ch sp, *sc in next ch sp, (2 dc, ch 2, 2 dc) in next ch sp; repeat from * around, join. Fasten off.♦

Striped Delight Pillow

continued from page 103

continued from page 103

For **center,** working in starting ch on opposite side of row 1, join black with sc in first ch, 3 sc in next ch, sc in last ch. Fasten off.

Matching centers and ends of rows, sew four Panels together forming a square. Sew white button to center.

SIDE B

Work same as Side A, reversing colors.

ASSEMBLY

Holding Sides wrong sides together, working through both thicknesses, holding one strand each black and white together, join with sc in any st, sc in each st around inserting pillow form before closing, join with sl st in first sc. Fasten off.♦

Caution: Place rug in low-traffic area of your home or spray with rug backing to eliminate the possibility of slipping.

Victorian Rug

Designed by Carolyn Christmas

Add a touch of old-time charm to any room or hallway with this simple little rug stitched in a velvety-soft combination of chunky chenille and cotton yarns.

FINISHED SIZE: 19" x 28½".

MATERIALS: 200 yds. burgundy chunky chenille yarn; 200 yds. blue cotton chunky yarn; Crochenit™ hook.

GAUGE: 4 corn sts = 5"; 7 rows = 2".

SPECIAL STITCH: For **corn st,** pull up lp in first ch of next ch-3, insert hook under top strand of 2 horizontal bars above next shell 3 rows below, yo, pull lp through, ch 1, pull up lp in last ch of same ch-3.

CROCHENIT™ STITCH: Corn Stitch #305

NOTE: Read General Instructions on page 8 before beginning pattern.

CAUTION: Place rug in low-traffic area of your home or spray with rug backing to eliminate the possibility of slipping.

RUG

Row 1: With cotton yarn, ch 43, pull up lp in second ch from hook, pull up lp in each ch across, turn. *(43 lps on hook)*

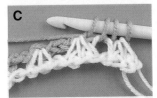

Row 2: With chenille yarn, yo, pull through first lp on hook, yo, pull through 4 lps on hook *(this completes a ch-1 and a shell—see photo A),* *ch 2, yo, pull through 4 lps on hook *(this completes a ch-3 and a shell—see photo B);* repeat from * across, **do not turn.**

Row 3: Ch 1, skip first shell, pull up lp in first ch of next ch-3, insert hook in ch directly below on row 1, yo, pull

lp through, ch 1, pull up lp in last ch of same ch-3 *(this completes a corn st—see photo C),* *skip next shell, pull up lp in first ch of next ch-3, insert hook in ch directly below on row 1, yo, pull lp through, ch 1, pull up lp in last ch of same ch-3 *(this completes a corn st);* repeat from * 11 more times, skip last shell, pull up lp in last ch, turn. *(41 lps on hook)*

Row 4: With cotton yarn, yo, pull through first lp on hook, *ch 2, yo, pull through 4 lps on hook *(this completes a ch-3 and a shell);* repeat from * 12 more times, ch 2, yo, pull through 2 lps on hook *(this completes a ch-3),* **do not turn.**

Row 5: Ch 1, **corn st** *(see Special Stitch),* (skip next shell on this row, corn st) 13 times, turn. *(43 lps on hook)*

Row 6: With chenille yarn, yo, pull through first lp on hook, yo, pull through 4 lps on hook *(this completes a ch-1 and a shell),* *ch 2, yo, pull through 4 lps on hook *(this completes a ch-3 and a shell);* repeat from * across, **do not turn.**

Row 7: Ch 1, skip first shell, corn st, (skip next shell on this row, corn st) 12 times, skip last shell on this row, pull up lp in last ch, turn. *(41 lps on hook)*

Rows 8-88: Repeat rows 4-7 consecutively, ending with row 4.

Row 89: Ch 1, sl st in first ch of next ch-3, sc under top strand of 2 horizontal bars above first shell 3 rows below, sl st in last ch of same ch-3, (skip next shell on this row, sl st in first ch of next ch-3, sc under top strand of 2 horizontal bars above next shell 3 rows below, sl st in last ch of same ch-3) across. Fasten off.

BORDER

Rnd 1: Working in rnds, join cotton yarn with sc in first row before either long edge, *evenly spacing sts so piece lays flat, sc in ends of rows across; working across short end, 5 dc in top of next chenille st, (sl st in top of next chenille st, 5 dc in top of next chenille st) across; repeat from * one more time, join with sl st in first sc. Fasten off.♦

Potpourri Basket

DESIGNED BY SUE PENROD

Fill this decorative basket with little treasures for safekeeping or with fragrant potpourri to freshen any room in your home!

FINISHED SIZE: 4½" tall x 5" across.

MATERIALS: Plastic canvas worsted yarn—2 oz. each off-white and beige; large wooden bead; thin strip of leather; 1 cup *(8 oz.)* round plastic storage container; craft glue or hot glue gun; tapestry needle; H double-ended hook or hook size needed to obtain gauge.

GAUGE: 4 sts = 1"; 12 rows = 1".

NOTE: Read General Instructions on page 6 before beginning pattern.

BASKET
Bottom

Row 1: With beige, ch 9, pull up lp in second ch from hook, pull up lp in each ch across, turn. *(9 lps on hook)*

Row 2: With off-white, work lps off hook, **do not turn.**

Row 3: Ch 1, skip first vertical bar, pull up lp under each **horizontal bar** *(see illustration)* across, turn.

Horizontal Bar

Row 4: With beige, work lps off hook, **do not turn.**

Row 5: Ch 1, skip first vertical bar, pull up lp under each horizontal bar across, turn.

Rows 6-120: Repeat rows 2-5 consecutively, ending with row 4.

Row 121: Ch 1, skip first vertical bar, sl st under each horizontal bar across, **do not turn; to gather bottom of Basket,** ch 1, pull up lp in end of every other row across, yo, pull through all lps on hook, ch 1. Leaving long

end for sewing, fasten off. Sew first and last rows together.

Sides

Row 1: With beige, ch 12, pull up lp in second ch from hook, pull up lp in each ch across, turn. *(12 lps on hook)*

Row 2: With off-white, work lps off hook, **do not turn.**

Row 3: Ch 1, skip first vertical bar, pull up lp under each horizontal bar across, turn.

Row 4: With beige, work lps off hook, **do not turn.**

Row 5: Ch 1, skip first vertical bar, pull up lp under each horizontal bar across, turn.

Rows 6-180: Repeat rows 2-5 consecutively, ending with row 4.

Row 181: Ch 1, skip first vertical bar, sl st under each horizontal bar across. Leaving long end for sewing, fasten off. Sew first and last rows together.

Easing to fit, sew Sides and Bottom together.

Glue plastic container inside Basket Bottom. For **drawstring,** with tapestry needle, weave long strand of beige through ends of rows at top of Basket. Pull ends of yarn tight to gather, tie into a bow.

LID

Row 1: With beige, ch 6, pull up lp in second ch from hook, pull up lp in each ch across, turn. *(6 lps on hook)*

Row 2: With off-white, work lps off hook, **do not turn.**

Row 3: Ch 1, skip first vertical bar, pull up lp under each horizontal bar across, turn.

Row 4: With beige, work lps off hook, **do not turn.**

Row 5: Ch 1, skip first vertical bar, pull up lp under each horizontal bar across, turn.

Rows 6-96: Repeat rows 2-5 consecutively, *continued on page 113*

Paradise Afghan

DESIGNED BY CHRISTINE GRAZIOSO

The rich, vivid hues of an exotic garden create the colorful panorama of this beautiful afghan. Bright, cheery blocks of color are actually easy-to-make panels that are worked continuously, then edged in black to create a dramatic effect.

FINISHED SIZES: 40" x 64½".

MATERIALS: 18 oz. of various colors of light and dark scrap and 11 oz. black worsted yarn; tapestry needle; I crochet hook and J double-ended hooks or hook size needed to obtain gauge.

GAUGE: With **double-ended hook,** 7 sts = 2"; 4 pattern rows = 1". Each Panel is 4" wide x 63" long not including Edging.

SPECIAL STITCH: For **tr lp,** yo 2 times, insert hook in bar specified in instructions, yo, pull through, (yo, pull through 2 lps on hook) 2 times.

NOTES: Read General Instructions on page 6 before beginning pattern.

Use double-ended hook unless otherwise stated.

AFGHAN
Panel (make 3)

Row 1: With dark scrap color, ch 15, pull up lp in second ch from hook, pull up lp in next ch, ***tr lp** in next ch (*see Special Stitch*), pull up lp in next 3 chs; repeat from * across, turn. (*15 lps on hook*)

Row 2: With light scrap color, work lps off hook, **do not turn.**

Row 3: Ch 1, pull up lp in top strand of next 2 **horizontal bars** (*see illustration*), (tr in top strand of next horizontal bar, pull up lp in top strand of next 3 horizontal bars) across, turn.

Horizontal Bar

Row 4: With same dark color, work lps off hook, **do not turn.**

Row 5: Ch 1, pull up lp in top strand of next 2 horizontal bars, (tr in top strand of next horizontal bar, pull up lp in top strand of next 3 horizontal bars) across, turn.

Row 6: With same light color, work lps off hook, **do not turn.**

Row 7: Ch 1, pull up lp in top strand of next 2 horizontal bars, (tr lp in top strand of next horizontal bar, pull up lp in top strand of next 3 horizontal bars) across, turn.

Rows 8-27: Repeat rows 4-7 consecutively.

Row 28: With next dark scrap color, work lps off hook, **do not turn.**

Row 29: Ch 1, pull up lp in top strand of next 2 horizontal bars, (tr lp in top strand of next horizontal bar, pull up lp in top strand of next 3 horizontal bas) across, turn.

Row 30: With next light scrap color, work lps off hook, **do not turn.**

Row 31: Ch 1, pull up lp in top strand of next 2 horizontal bars, (tr lp in top strand of next horizontal bar, pull up lp in top strand of next 3 horizontal bars) across, turn.

Row 32: With same dark scrap color, work lps off hook, **do not turn.**

Row 33: Ch 1, pull up lp in top strand of next 2 horizontal bars, (tr lp in top strand of next horizontal bar, pull up lp in top strand of next 3 horizontal bars) across, turn.

Row 34: With same light scrap color, work lps off hook, **do not turn.**

Row 35: Ch 1, pull up lp in top strand of next 2 horizontal bars, (tr lp in top strand of next horizontal bar, pull up lp in top strand of next 3 horizontal bars) across, turn.

Rows 36-55: Repeat rows 32-35 consecutively.

Rows 56-251: Repeat rows 28-55 consecutively.

Row 252: With same light scrap color, work lps off hook. Fasten off.

First Side Edging

Row 1: With I hook and predominately light color side facing you, working in ends of rows across one long edge, join black with sl st in last

continued on page 113

Microwave Mitt

Designed by Debbie Tabor

Microwave cooking will never be too hot to handle with this clever little oven mitt that's quickly stitched with only a small amount of worsted yarn on a large-size hook.

FINISHED SIZE: 5" x 7" not including hanging loop.

MATERIALS: Worsted yarn—1½ oz. each dk. green and lt. green, small amount brown; 4" square piece red felt; red and white sewing thread; sewing and tapestry needles; J double-ended hook or hook size needed to obtain gauge.

GAUGE: 4 sts = 1"; 7 rows = 1".

NOTE: Read General Instructions on page 6 before beginning pattern.

MITT

Row 1: With dk. green, ch 20, pull up lp in second ch from hook, pull up lp in each ch across, turn. *(20 lps on hook)*

Row 2: With lt. green, work lps off hook, **do not turn.**

Row 3: Ch 1, skip first vertical bar, pull up lp in top strand of each **hori-**

Horizontal Bar

zontal bar across *(see illustration)*, turn.

Row 4: With dk. green, work lps off hook, **do not turn.**

Row 5: Ch 1, skip first vertical bar, pull up lp in top strand of each horizontal bar across, turn.

Rows 6-104: Repeat rows 2-5 consecutively, ending with row 4.

Row 105: Ch 1, skip first vertical bar, sl st in top strand of each horizontal bar across. Fasten off.

For **hanging loop,** join dk. green with sl st in end of row at center of one long edge, ch 12, sl st in same row. Fasten off. Secure ends.

With predominantly lt. green side of piece facing you, fold 4" on short ends toward center. Sew together at each edge forming pockets.

Cut two apples from red felt according to pattern. With sewing thread, sew apple in place.

With brown, using straight stitch *(see illustration)*, embroider one **stem** over each apple. With white sewing thread, embroider **sparkle** to one corner of each apple as shown in photo.♦

Apple Pattern

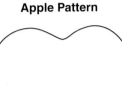

Straight Stitch

Potpourri Basket
continued from page 109

ending with row 4.

Row 97: Ch 1, skip first vertical bar, sl st under each horizontal bar across; to **gather center of Lid,** ch 1, pull up lp in end of every other row across, yo, pull through all lps on hook, ch 1. Leaving long end for sewing, fasten off. Sew first and last rows together.

Attach wooden bead to center of Lid with leather strip. With tapestry needle and off-white, whipstitch around outer edge of Lid.

If desired, with off-white, using chain stitch *(see illustration),* embroider top of Lid and Basket Sides as shown in photo.♦

Chain Stitch

Paradise Afghan
continued from page 111

row, ch 3, evenly space 188 dc across, turn. *(189 dc made)*

Row 2: Ch 4, skip next st, dc in next st, (ch 1, skip next st, dc in next st) across, turn.

Row 3: Ch 3, dc in each ch sp and in each st across. Fasten off.

Second Side Edging
Working on opposite long edge of same

Panel, starting in row 1, work same as First Side Edging.

Assembly
Matching sts on long edges, sew Panels together.

End Edging
With right side facing you, using I hook and black, starting at top right corner, join with sl st in end of row 3 on Side Edging, ch 3, evenly space 131 dc across. Fasten off.

Repeat End Edging on opposite end.♦

Monk's Cloth Place Mat

DESIGNED BY ELEANOR ALBANO-MILES

The beautiful woven design on both sides of this distinctive place mat makes it twice as nice and doubly decorative!

FINISHED SIZE: 12" x 16".

MATERIALS: Worsted yarn—7 oz. white, 3½ oz. each yellow, lt. gold, dk. gold, aqua, lt. teal, dk. teal and purple; craft glue or hot glue gun; tapestry needle; K double-ended and K crochet hook or hook sizes needed to obtain gauges.

GAUGES: With **double-ended hook,** 4 sts = 1"; 6 rows = 1". With **K hook,** 8 sc = 3".

NOTES: Read General Instructions on page 6 before beginning pattern.

Place Mat will require two separate skeins or balls of white.

PLACE MAT

Row 1: With double-ended hook and white, ch 41, pull up lp in second ch from hook, pull up lp in each ch across, turn. *(41 lps on hook)*

Row 2: With white, work lps off hook, **do not turn.**

Row 3: Ch 1, skip first vertical bar, pull up lp in each vertical bar across, turn.

Row 4: With white, work lps off hook, **do not turn.**

Row 5: Ch 1, skip first vertical bar, pull up lp in each vertical bar across, turn.

Rows 6-116: Repeat rows 2-5 consecutively, ending with row 4. At end of last row, fasten off.

WEAVING

Weave yarn through loops across the length of crocheted Place Mat, with colors and placement indicated on Graph A on page 119. To **secure yarn ends,** weave yarn back through

last 2 loops in the opposite direction forming a loop above the stitch. Remove needle. Protect work surface to prevent glue damage. Dab a small amount of glue to top of st under the loop, then pull loop tight. (Use paper towels to clean the tip of glue bottle frequently.) When dry, trim yarn close to glue. Repeat on all ends.

Weave other side of Place Mat in same manner according to Graph B on page 119.

BORDER

Rnd 1: Working around outer edge, with K hook and white, join with sc in first vertical bar of *continued on page 119*

Nine-Patch Afghan

DESIGNED BY JOYCE NORDSTROM

Worked in strips to create the traditional look of patchwork quilting, this charming afghan will add an old-fashioned touch to any room in the house.

FINISHED SIZE: 55" x 65".

MATERIALS: Worsted yarn—24 oz. variegated print, 18 oz. soft white, 16 oz. each of blue and tan; tapestry needle; K double-ended and J hooks or hook size needed to obtain gauge.

GAUGE: With **double-ended hook,** 4 sts = 1"; 6 rows = 1".

NOTES: Read General Instructions on page 6 before beginning pattern.

Use double-ended hook unless otherwise stated.

AFGHAN

Strip A (make 12)

Row 1: With print, ch 15, draw up lp in second ch from hook, draw up lp in each ch across, turn. *(15 lps on hook)*

Row 2: With blue, work lps off hook, **do not turn.**

Row 3: Ch 1, skip first vertical bar, draw up lp in each vertical bar across, turn.

Row 4: With print, work lps off hook, **do not turn.**

Row 5: Ch 1, skip first vertical bar, draw up lp in each vertical bar across, turn.

Rows 6-27: Repeat rows 2-5 consecutively, ending with row 3. **Fasten off print and blue.**

Row 28: With soft white, work lps off hook, **do not turn.**

Row 29: Ch 1, skip first vertical bar, draw up lp in each vertical bar across, turn.

Row 30: With tan, work lps off hook, **do not turn.**

Row 31: Ch 1, skip first vertical bar, draw up lp in each vertical bar across, turn.

Rows 32-53: Repeat rows 28-31 consecutively, ending with row 33. **Fasten off soft white and tan.**

Row 54: With print, work lps off hook, **do not turn.**

Row 55: Ch 1, skip first vertical bar, draw up lp in each vertical bar across, turn.

Rows 56-78: Repeat rows 2-5, ending with row 4. At end of last row, fasten off.

Strip B (make 20)

Row 1: With soft white, ch 15, draw up lp in second ch from hook, draw up lp in each ch across, turn. *(15 lps on hook)*

Row 2: With tan, work lps off hook, **do not turn.**

Row 3: Ch 1, skip first vertical bar, draw up lp in each vertical bar across, turn.

Row 4: With soft white, work lps off hook, **do not turn.**

Row 5: Ch 1, skip first vertical bar, draw up lp in each vertical bar across, turn.

Rows 6-27: Repeat rows 2-5 consecutively, ending with row 3. **Fasten off soft white and tan.**

Row 28: With print, work lps off hook, **do not turn.**

Row 29: Ch 1, skip first vertical bar, draw up lp in each vertical bar across, turn.

Row 30: With blue, work lps off hook, **do not turn.**

Row 31: Ch 1, skip first vertical bar, draw up lp in each vertical bar across, turn.

Rows 32-53: Repeat rows 28-31 consecutively, ending with row 33. **Fasten off print and blue.**

Row 54: With soft white, work lps off hook, **do not turn.**

Row 55: Ch 1, skip first vertical bar, draw up lp in each vertical bar across, turn.

Rows 56-78: Repeat rows 2-5, ending with row 4. At end of last row, fasten off.

Sew three Strips together alternating Strips according to illustration on page 118, making eight large blocks. Sew two Strips together making four small blocks.

Large Block (make 3 print/blue and 4 soft white/tan)

Row 1: With print or soft white, ch 45, draw up lp in second ch from hook, draw up lp in each ch across, turn. *(45 lps on hook)*

Row 2: With blue or tan, work lps off hook, **do not turn.**

Row 3: Ch 1, skip first vertical bar, draw up lp in each vertical bar across, turn.

Row 4: With print or soft white, work lps off hook, **do not turn.**

Row 5: Ch 1, skip first vertical bar, draw up lp in each vertical bar across, turn.

Rows 6-78: Repeat rows 2-5 consecutively, ending with row 4. At end of last row, fasten off.

Medium Block (make 6)

Row 1: With print, ch 30, draw up lp in second ch from hook, draw up lp in each ch across, turn. *(30 lps on hook)*

Row 2: With blue, work lps off hook, **do not turn.**

Row 3: Ch 1, skip first vertical bar, draw up lp in each vertical bar across, turn.

Row 4: With print, work lps off hook, **do not turn.**

Row 5: Ch 1, skip first vertical bar, draw up lp in each vertical bar across, turn.

Rows 6-78: Repeat rows 2-5 consecutively, ending with row 4. At end of last row, fasten off.

Edging

Working around outer edge of Blocks or assembled Stripes, working in ends of rows, in sts or in starting ch on opposite side of row 1, join print with sc in any corner, working from left to right, ch 1, skip next row, **reverse sc** *(see Stitch Guide on page 11)* in next row, (ch 1, skip next st or next row, reverse sc in next st or row) around, join with sl st in first sc. Fasten off.

Sew assembled Strips and Blocks together according to illustration.

BORDER

Rnd 1: Working around entire outer edge, join soft white with sc in ch sp at any corner, working from left to right, (ch 1, reverse sc) in same ch sp, ch 1, (reverse sc, ch 1) in each ch sp around with (sc, ch 1, sc, ch 1) in each corner, join with sl st in first sc. Fasten off.

Rnd 2: Join print with sc in any corner ch sp, ch 1, reverse sc in same ch sp, ch 1, (reverse sc, ch 1) in each ch sp around with (sc, ch 1, sc, ch 1) in each corner ch sp, join with sl st in first sc. Fasten off.♦

Monk's Cloth
Place Mat
continued from page 115

last row, ch 2, sc in same sp, sc in each vertical bar across to last vertical bar, (sc, ch 2, sc) in last vertical bar; working in ends of rows, sc evenly spaced across; working in starting ch on opposite side of row 1, (sc, ch 2, sc) in first ch, sc in each ch across with (sc, ch 2, sc) in last ch; working in ends of rows, sc evenly spaced across, join with sl st in first sc, **turn**. Fasten off.

Rnd 2: Join dk. gold with sc in any corner ch sp, ch 2, sc in same sp, sc in each st around with (sc, ch 2, sc) in each corner ch sp, join, **turn**.

Rnd 3: Ch 1, sc in each st around with (sc, ch 2, sc) in each corner ch sp, join. Fasten off.♦

Color Key
| = Yellow (A)
| = Lt. Gold (B)
| = Dk. Gold (C)
| = Aqua (D)
| = Lt. Teal (E)
| = Dk. Teal (F)
| = Purple (G)

Graph A

Graph B

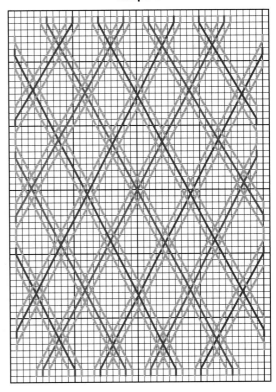

Wonderful
Wraps

Chapter
Four

Monoghan Poncho

DESIGNED BY JOYCE NORDSTROM

Double your poncho pleasure with a pattern that's reversible in both color and design! Crochet this versatile fashion accent in vibrant or muted shades to compliment your wardrobe or to reflect the mood of your day!

FINISHED SIZE: Instructions given fit size small/medium. Changes for large/extra-large are in [ ].

MATERIALS: Worsted yarn—12 [14] oz. each gray and white; stitch markers; tapestry needle; K double-ended and I crochet hooks or hook size needed to obtain gauge.

GAUGE: With **double-ended hook,** 7 sts = 2"; 12 pattern rows = 2¾"

SPECIAL STITCHES: For **sc lp,** pull up lp in specified bar or st, yo, pull through one lp on hook.

For **tr lp,** yo 2 times, insert hook in specified st or bar, yo, pull lp through, (yo, pull through 2 lps on hook) 2 times. Skip next vertical bar on last row behind tr lp.

For **double treble crochet front post lp (dtr fp lp),** yo 3 times, insert hook from front to back around post of specified st, yo, pull lp through, (yo, pull through 2 lps on hook) 3 times. Skip next vertical bar on last row behind dtr fp lp.

For **gray cable,** skip first post st of next 2 post st group, dtr fp lp around next post st, pull up lp in next 2 vertical bars on last row, dtr fp lp around skipped post st.

For **white cable,** skip first post st of next 2 post st group, dtr fp lp around next post st, sc lp in next 2 vertical bars on last row, dtr fp lp around skipped post st.

For **double treble crochet front post (dtr fp),** yo 3 times, insert

hook from front to back around post of specified st, yo, pull lp through, (yo, pull through 2 lps on hook) 4 times. Skip next vertical bar on last row behind post st.

NOTE: Read General Instructions on page 6 before beginning pattern.

PANEL (make 2)

Row 1: With double-ended hook and gray, ch 78, pull up lp in second ch from hook, pull up lp in each ch across, turn. *(78 lps on hook)*

Row 2: With white, work lps off hook, **do not turn.**

continued on page 128

Capelet & Pouch

DESIGNED BY ANN PARNELL

Stitched in double strands of metallic thread, this beautiful capelet and matching little drawstring purse will dress up any evening ensemble with glamorous sparkle!

FINISHED SIZES: Instructions given for Capelet are for small/medium. Changes for large/extra large are in [ ]. Pouch is 4" x 5" not including drawstrings.

MATERIALS FOR CAPELET: Size 10 metallic crochet thread—800 yds. each ecru and gold; tapestry needle; H double-ended hook or hook size needed to obtain gauge.

MATERIALS FOR POUCH: Size 10 metallic crochet thread—200 yds. each ecru and gold; (optional: 13½" circle of lightweight lining fabric); tapestry needle; H double-ended and E crochet hooks or hook size needed to obtain gauge.

GAUGE: With **double-ended hook and two strands held together,** 5 shells = 3"; 6 shell rows = 1".

NOTES: Read General Instructions on page 6 before beginning pattern.

Use two strands same color thread held together as one unless otherwise stated.

CAPELET

Row 1: With ecru, ch 63, pull up lp in second ch from hook, pull up lp in each ch across, turn. *(63 lps on hook)*

Row 2: With gold, pull through first lp on hook, ch 1, yo, pull through 4 lps on hook *(completes a ch-2 and a shell),* *ch 2, yo, pull through 4 lps on hook, *(completes a ch-3 and a shell);* repeat from * across to last 6 lps on hook, ch 1; for **neck ribbing,** (yo, pull through 2 lps on hook) 5 times, **do not turn.** *(19 shells)*

Row 3: Skip first vertical bar, pull up lp under each of next 5 **horizontal bars** *(see illustration),* skip next shell, (pull up lp in **top strand**

Horizontal Bar

of next 3 chs, skip next shell) across to last ch sp, pull up lp in **top strand** of last 2 chs, turn. *(62 lps on hook)*

Row 4: With ecru, pull through first lp on hook; for **neck ribbing,** yo, pull through 2 lps on hook) 5 times, *ch 2, yo, pull through 4 lps on hook *(completes a ch-3 and a shell);* repeat from * across to last 3 lps on hook, ch 2, yo, pull through last 3 lps on hook *(completes a ch-3 and a shell),* **do not turn.**

Row 5: Ch 1, skip first shell, (pull up lp in **top strand** of next 3 chs) across to last 5 horizontal bars, pull up lp under each of last 5 horizontal bars, turn. *(63 lps on hook)*

Rows 6-340 [6-376]: Repeat rows 2-5 consecutively, ending with row 4. At end of last row, leaving long end for sewing, fasten off. Matching sts, sew first and last rows together.

Optional: Capelet is designed to have a low neckline. If a tighter neckline is desired, make a drawstring as follows: with one strand each color held together, ch 240 or to desired length, sl st in second ch from hook, sl st in each ch across. Fasten off. Weave through ends of rows at top of neck ribbing. Pull up to gather and tie ends into a bow.

POUCH

Row 1: With double-ended hook and ecru, ch 30, pull up lp in second ch from hook, pull up lp in each ch across, turn. *(30 lps on hook)*

Rows 2-92: Repeat rows 2-5 of Capelet consecutively, ending with row 4. *(Neck ribbing will form mouth of Pouch.)* At end of last row, leaving long end for sewing, fasten off. Matching sts, using a single strand of ecru, sew first and last rows together. For **bottom,** with two strands of gold held together, weave through ends of gold rows on bottom of Pouch. Pull tight to gather, secure ends.

For **drawstring** (make 2), with E hook and one strand each ecru and gold held together, ch 120, *continued on page 128*

Butterfly Cape

DESIGNED BY PRISCILLA COLE

Plush, ribbed stripes create the striking pattern in this marvelous, oversized design in creative cover-ups. Simple hook closures add the finishing touch.

FINISHED SIZE: One size fits all.

MATERIALS: Worsted yarn—24 oz. each main color (MC) and contrasting color (CC); 4 black thread-covered large coat hooks and eyes; safety pins; tapestry needle; I double-ended hook or hook size needed to obtain gauge.

GAUGE: 14 sts = 4"; 6 rows = 1".

NOTES: Read General Instructions on page 6 before beginning pattern.

SIDE (make one as written; make one reversing colors)

Row 1: Starting at **bottom front corner,** with MC, ch 4, pull up lp in second ch from hook, pull up lp in each ch across, turn. *(4 lps on hook)*

Row 2: With CC, work lps off hook, **do not turn.**

Row 3: Skip first vertical bar, pull up lp in top strand of each **horizontal bar** across *(see illustration),* pull up lp in last vertical bar, turn. *(5)*

Horizontal Bar

Row 4: With MC, work lps off hook, **do not turn.**

Row 5: Skip first vertical bar, pull up lp in top strand of each horizontal bar across, pull up lp in last vertical bar, turn. *(6)*

Rows 6-199: Repeat rows 2-5 consecutively, ending with row 3 and *103 lps on hook* in last row.

Row 200: With MC, work lps off hook, **do not turn.**

Row 201: Skip first vertical bar, pull up lp in top strand of each horizontal bar across, turn.

Row 202: With CC, work lps off hook, **do not turn.**

Row 203: Skip first vertical bar, pull up lp in top strand of each horizontal bar across, turn.

Rows 204-222: Repeat rows 200-203, ending with row 202.

Row 223: Skip first vertical bar, pull up lp in top strand of next 93 horizontal bars leaving remaining horizontal bars unworked for **collar,** turn. *(94)*

Row 224: With MC, work lps off hook, **do not turn.**

Row 225: Skip first vertical bar, skip next horizontal bar, pull up lp in top strand of each horizontal bar across, turn. *(93)*

Row 226: With CC, work lps off hook, **do not turn.**

Row 227: Skip first vertical bar, skip next horizontal bar, pull up lp in top strand of each horizontal bar across, turn. *(92)*

Rows 228-403: Repeat rows 222-225 consecutively, ending with *4 lps on hook* in last row.

Row 404: With MC, work lps off hook. Fasten off.

For **center back seam,** with predominantly MC side of each Side facing you, using MC, sew unworked sts of row 223 and ends of rows 224-404 together.

BORDER STRIP (make one as written; make one reversing colors)

Row 1: With CC, ch 3, pull up lp in second ch from hook, pull up lp in last ch, turn. *(3 lps on hook)*

Row 2: With MC, work lps off hook, **do not turn.**

Row 3: Ch 2, pull up lp in second ch from hook, pull up lp in top strand of each horizontal bar across, turn. *(4 lps on hook)*

Row 4: With CC, work lps off hook, **do not turn.**

Row 5: Skip first vertical bar, pull up lp in top strand of each horizontal bar across, pull up lp in last vertical bar, turn. *(5)*

Rows 6-19: Repeat rows 2-5 consecutively, ending with *12 lps on hook* in last row.

Row 20: With MC, work lps off hook, **do not turn.**

Row 21: Skip first vertical bar, pull up lp in top strand of each horizontal bar across, turn.

Row 22: With CC, work lps off hook, **do not turn.**

Row 23: Skip first vertical bar, pull up lp in top strand of each horizontal bar across, turn.

Rows 24-484: Repeat rows 20-23 consecutively, ending with row 20.

Row 485: Skip first vertical bar, skip next horizontal bar, pull up lp in top strand of each horizontal bar across, turn. *(11)*

Row 486: With CC, work lps off hook, **do not turn.**

Row 487: Skip first vertical bar, pull up lp in top strand of each horizontal bar across leaving last horizontal bar unworked, turn. *(10)*

Row 488: With MC, work lps off hook, **do not turn.**

Rows 489-501: Repeat rows 485-488 consecutively, ending with row 485 and *3 lps on hook* in last row.

Row 502: With CC, yo, pull through all lps on hook. Fasten off.

Holding Cape with predominantly MC side facing you and one Border Strip with predominantly CC side facing you and held together as

shown in diagram, pin first row after increases of Border Strip to bottom point of Cape, pin last row before decreases to opposite bottom point on Cape, pin center of Border Strip to center of Cape; working in ends of rows, join MC with sc in first row at bottom point of cape, ch 1, sc in next row on Border Strip; adjusting sts if necessary so Cape lays flat and easing to fit, (ch 1, skip next 2 or 3 rows on Cape, sc in next row, ch 1, skip next 2 or 3 rows on Border Strip, sc in next row) across. Fasten off.

Join other Border Strip to opposite side of Cape in same manner; continue to crochet ends of Border Strips together below center back seam.

Try on Cape turning back collar as shown in photo. Place safety pins on each side where top coat hook and eye will comfortably fasten. Remove Cape. Sew first hook and eye at safety pin markers; sew remaining hooks spaced 3½" apart.♦

Capelet & Pouch
continued from page 125

sl st in second ch from hook, sl st in each ch across. Fasten off. Starting at seam, weave one drawstring through rows 1" below mouth of Pouch. Knot ends. Starting at opposite side, weave remaining drawstring in opposite direction. Knot ends.

Optional: For **lining,** sew a ¼" hem around fabric circle. Hand baste around circle and pull ends to gather to about same size as Pouch. Insert inside Pouch and tack in place just below drawstrings.♦

Monoghan Poncho
continued from page 123

Row 3: Ch 1, skip first vertical bar, **sc lp** *(see Special Stitches)* in each vertical bar across, turn.

Row 4: With gray, work lps off hook, **do not turn.**

Row 5: Ch 1, skip first vertical bar, pull up lp in next 9 vertical bars,* **tr lp** *(see Special Stitches)* in corresponding st on row 2, pull up lp in next 2 vertical bars on last row, skip next 2 sts on row 2, tr lp in next st, pull up lp in next 4 vertical bars on last row, tr lp in corresponding st on row 2, pull up lp in next 2 vertical bars on last row, skip next 2 sts on row 2, tr lp in next st*, pull up lp in next 34 vertical bars on last row; repeat between **, pull up lp in last 10 vertical bars on last row, turn.

Row 6: With white, work lps off hook, **do not turn.**

Row 7: Ch 1, skip first vertical bar, sc lp in next 9 vertical bars, *tr lp in vertical bar of corresponding st 4 rows below, sc lp in next 2 vertical bars on last row, skip next 2 sts 4 rows below, tr lp in vertical bar of next st, sc lp in next 4 vertical bars on last row, tr lp in vertical bar of corresponding st 4 rows below, sc lp in next 2 vertical bars of last row, skip next 2 sts 4 rows below, tr lp in next st*, sc lp in next 34 vertical bars on last row; repeat between **, sc lp in last 10 vertical bars on last row, turn.

Row 8: With gray, work lps off hook, **do not turn.**

Row 9: Ch 1, skip first vertical bar, pull up lp in next 9 vertical bars, *work **gray cable** *(see Special Stitches),* pull up lp in next 4 vertical bars, work gray cable*, pull up lp in next 34 vertical bars; repeat between **, pull up lp in last 10 vertical bars, turn.

Row 10: With white, work lps off hook, **do not turn.**

Row 11: Ch 1, skip first vertical bar, sc lp in next 9 vertical bars, *work **white cable** *(see Special Stitches),* sc lp in next 4 vertical bars, work white cable*, sc lp in next 34 vertical bars; repeat between **, sc lp in last 10 vertical bars, turn.

Row 12: With gray, work lps off hook, **do not turn.**

Row 13: Ch 1, skip first vertical bar, pull up lp in next 9 vertical bars, *tr lp around post of first st of next 2-post st group, pull up lp in next 2 vertical bars on last row, tr lp around post of next st of same group, pull up lp in next 4 vertical bars on last row, tr lp around post of first st of next 2-post st group, pull up lp in next 2 vertical bars on last row, tr lp around post of next st of same group*, pull up lp in next 34 vertical bars on last row; repeat between **, pull up lp in last 10 vertical bars on last row, turn.

Row 14: With white, work lps off hook, **do not turn.**

Row 15: Ch 1, skip first vertical bar, sc lp in next 9 vertical bars, *tr lp around post of first st of next 2-post st group, sc lp in next 2 vertical bars on last row, tr lp around post of next st of same group, sc lp in next 4 vertical bars on last row, tr lp around post of first st of next 2-post st group, sc lp in next 2 vertical bars on last row, tr lp around post of next st of same group*, sc lp in next 34 vertical bars on last row; repeat between **, sc lp in last 10 vertical bars on last row, turn.

Rows 16-122 [16-130]: Repeat rows 8-15 consecutively, ending with row 10.

Row 123 [131]: Sl st in first 10 vertical bars, **dtr fp around post of second st of next 2-post st group, sl st in next 2 vertical bars on last row, dtr fp around post of first st of same group, sl st in next 4 vertical bars on last row, dtr fp around post of second st of next 2-post st group, sl st in next 2 vertical bars on last row, dtr fp around post of first st of same group*, sl st in next 34 vertical bars on last row; repeat between **, sl st in last 10 vertical bars on last row. Fasten off.

ASSEMBLY

With predominantly gray side of Panels facing you, place stitch marker 7" [8½"] below upper right corner on each Panel. Place end of second Panel against side of first Panel, *(see letters A on assembly illustration).* Working through both thicknesses and easing to fit, with I hook and gray, join with sc in first st to the left; working from left to right, (ch 1, skip next st, **reverse sc** in next st—*see Stitch Guide)* across. Fasten off.

Place end of first Panel against side of second Panel *(see letters B on assembly illustration),* join in same manner stopping at marker. **Do not fasten off.** Working in sts and in ends of rows around neck opening, evenly spacing sts so piece lays flat, (ch 1, skip next st or row, reverse sc in next st or row) around, sl st in seam. Fasten off.♦

Assembly Illustration

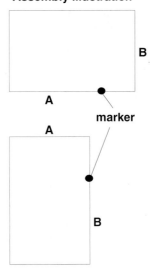

Lacy Stole

DESIGNED BY MARY MIDDLETON

Drape your shoulders in lacy elegance with this delicately-styled, worsted yarn stole that shimmers with edgings worked in glittering thread.

FINISHED SIZE: 17" x 60" not including Fringe.

MATERIALS: 8 oz. white worsted yarn; 300 yds. white/gold metallic size 10 crochet cotton thread; Crochenit™ hook.

GAUGE: 3 very fancy sts = 2"; 4 rows = 1½".

CROCHENIT™ STITCHES: High Stitch #104, Very Fancy Stitch #208

SPECIAL STITCHES: For **high st,** insert hook in next vertical bar or specified st, yo, pull lp through, ch 1.

For **very fancy st,** yo, insert hook in next 2 vertical bars at same time, yo, pull lp through, ch 1.

NOTES: Read General Instructions and Crochenit™ Tips on page 8 before beginning pattern.

Yarn side is right side of work.

STOLE

Row 1: With yarn, ch 49, pull up lp in third ch from hook, ch 1 *(high st made),* **high st** *(see Special Stitches)* in each ch across, turn. *(48 lps on hook)*

Row 2: With thread, work lps off hook, **do not turn.**

Row 3: Ch 1, skip first vertical bar, **very fancy st** *(see Special Stitches)* across to last vertical bar, high st in last vertical bar, turn.

Row 4: With yarn, work lps off hook, **do not turn.**

Row 5: Ch 1, skip first vertical bar, very fancy st across to last vertical bar, high st in last vertical bar, turn.

Rows 6-160: Repeat rows 2-5 consecutively, ending with row 4.

Row 161: Ch 1, sc in first vertical bar, (2 sc in next 2 vertical bars at same time) across to last vertical bar, sc in last vertical bar. Fasten off. *(48 sc)*

First Side Trim

Row 1: Join yarn with sc in end of row 161, evenly space 113 more sc in ends of rows across ending at row 1, **do not turn.** Fasten off.

Row 2: Join thread with sc in first st, sc in each st across. Fasten off.

Second Side Trim

Row 1: Join yarn with sc in end of row 1 on other side of Stole, evenly space 113 more sc in ends of rows across ending at row 161, **do not turn.** Fasten off.

Row 2: Join thread with sc in first st, sc in each st across. Fasten off.

FRINGE

For **each corner Fringe,** cut three strands of yarn and two strands of thread each 12" long; holding all strands together, fold in half, insert hook in st at corner, pull fold through, pull all loose ends through fold, tighten. Trim ends.

For **each center Fringe,** cut two strands of yarn and one strand of thread each 12" long; holding all strands together, fold in half, insert hook in st, pull fold through, pull all loose ends through fold, tighten. Trim ends.

Work one corner Fringe in each corner and evenly space 23 center Fringes in sts between corners on short ends of Stole.♦

Caped Wonder

DESIGNED BY ANN PARNELL

Emerge in sophisticated style with this ultra-chic cape worked in an open, airy design that makes it the perfect wardrobe accessory for cool evenings out!

FINISHED SIZE: One size fits all.

MATERIALS: Acrylic sport yarn—13 oz. beige and 10 oz. off-white; stitch markers; tapestry needle; K double-ended and G crochet hooks or hook sizes needed to obtain gauges.

GAUGES: With **double-ended hook,** 4 shells = 4"; 16 rows = 3". With **G hook,** 4 sts = 1".

SPECIAL STITCHES: For **increase (inc),** pull up lp in top strand of next horizontal bar *(see Stitch Guide),* pull up lp in next vertical bar.

For **shell,** yo, pull through 5 lps on hook.

For **decrease (dec),** pull through first 2 lps on hook. Decrease counts as one vertical bar.

NOTE: Read General Instructions on page 6 before beginning pattern.

SIDE (make 2)

Row 1: Starting at **corner,** with double-ended hook and off-white, ch 5, pull up lp in second ch from hook, pull up lp in each ch across, turn. *(5 lps on hook)*

Row 2: With beige, pull through first lp on hook, ch 3, yo, pull through 4 lps on hook *(shell made),* ch 3, yo, pull through last 2 lps on hook, **do not turn.**

Row 3: Ch 2, pull up lp in second ch from hook, pull up lp in next 3 chs, skip next shell, pull up lp in last 3 chs, turn. *(8 lps on hook)*

Row 4: With off-white, pull through first lp on hook, (yo, pull through 2 lps on hook) across, **do not turn.**

Row 5: Skip first vertical bar, pull up lp in each vertical bar across to last 2 vertical bars, **inc** *(see Special Stitches)* in last 2 vertical bars, turn. *(10 lps on hook)*

Row 6: With beige, pull through first lp on hook, ch 3, **shell** *(see Special Stitches),* ch 4, shell, ch 3, yo, pull through last 2 lps on hook, **do not turn.**

Row 7: Ch 2, pull up lp in second ch from hook, pull up lp in next 3 chs, skip next shell, pull up lp in next 4 chs, skip next shell, pull up lp in last 3 chs, turn. *(12 lps on hook)*

Row 8: With off-white, pull through first lp on hook, (yo, pull through 2 lps on hook) across, **do not turn.**

Row 9: Skip first vertical bar, pull up lp in each vertical bar across to last 2 vertical bars, inc in last 2 vertical bars, turn. *(14 lps on hook)*

Row 10: With beige, pull through first lp on hook, ch 3, shell, (ch 4, shell) across to last 2 lps on hook, ch 3, yo, pull through last 2 lps on hook, **do not turn.**

Row 11: Ch 2, pull up lp in second ch from hook, pull up lp in next 3 chs, skip next shell, (pull up lp in next 4 chs, skip next shell) across to last 3 chs, pull up lp in last 3 chs, turn. *(16 lps on hook)*

Rows 12-77: Repeat rows 8-11 consecutively, ending with row 9 and *82 lps on hook* in last row.

Row 78: With beige, pull through first lp on hook, ch 3, shell, (ch 4, shell) across to last 2 lps on hook, ch 2, yo, pull through last 2 lps on hook, **do not turn.**

Row 79: Ch 1, pull up lp in next 2 chs, skip next shell, (pull up lp in next 4 chs, skip next shell) across to last 3 chs, pull up lp in last 3 chs, turn.

Row 80: With off-white, pull through first lp on hook, (yo, pull through 2 lps on hook) across, **do not turn.**

Row 81: Ch 1, skip first vertical bar, pull up lp in each vertical bar across, turn.

Row 82: With beige, pull through first lp on hook, ch 3, shell, (ch 4, shell) across to last 2 lps on hook, ch 2, yo, pull through last 2 lps on hook, **do not turn.**

Rows 83-203: Repeat rows 79-82 consecutively, ending with row 79.

Row 204: With off-white, **dec** *(see Special Stitches),* (yo, pull through 2 lps on hook) across, **do not turn.**

Row 205: Ch 1, skip first vertical bar, pull up lp in each vertical bar across leaving last dec unworked, turn. *(80 lps on hook)*

Row 206: With beige, pull through first lp on

continued on page 135

Grape Sherbet Ribbed Scarf

DESIGNED BY CAROLYN CHRISTMAS

Fluffy, nubby-textured yarn worked with double strands in a ribbed design creates a luxuriously thick and soft scarf that's a must-have for those extra-frosty winter days!

FINISHED SIZE: 8" wide x 62½" long not including Fringe.

MATERIALS: 10 oz. nubby novelty yarn; Crochenit™ hook.

GAUGE: 3 sts = 1½"; 6 rows = 1".

CROCHENIT™ STITCH: Basic Stitch #101

NOTES: Read General Instructions on page 8 before beginning pattern.

Use two strands yarn held together throughout unless otherwise stated

SCARF

Row 1: Ch 125, pull up lp in second ch from hook, pull up lp in each ch across, turn. *(125 lps on hook)*

Row 2: Work lps off hook, **do not turn.**

Row 3: Ch 1, skip first vertical bar, pull up lp under top strand of each **horizontal bar** *(see illustration)* across, turn.

Rows 4-48: Repeat rows 2-3 alternately, ending with row 2.

Row 49: Ch 1, skip first vertical bar, sl st in each vertical bar across. Fasten off.

Horizontal Bar

FRINGE

For **each Fringe**, cut four strands each 18" long. With all strands held together, fold in half, insert hook in end of row, pull fold through, pull all loose ends through fold, tighten. Trim ends.

Evenly space six Fringe across each short edge of Scarf.♦

Caped Wonder

continued from page 133

hook, ch 3, shell, (ch 4, shell) across to last 4 lps on hook, ch 2, yo, pull through last 4 lps on hook, **do not turn.**

Row 207: Ch 1, pull up lp in next 2 chs, skip next shell, (pull up lp in next 4 chs, skip next shell) across to last 3 chs, pull up lp in last 3 chs, turn. *(78 lps on hook)*

Rows 208-279: Repeat rows 204-207 consecutively, ending with *6 lps on hook* in last row.

Row 280: With off-white, dec, (yo, pull through 2 lps on hook) across, **do not turn.** *(5 lps on hook)*

Row 281: Sl st in each vertical bar across. Fasten off. Place stitch marker in end of row 78 after angled edge and in end of row 203 on same side.

For **center back seam,** with predominantly beige sides facing, sew increases on one piece to decreases on other piece *(see assembly illustration).*

EDGING

Rnd 1: Working around entire outer edge, with G hook and beige, join with sc in center back seam, evenly spacing sts so piece lays flat, sc around with 2 sc in each corner, **turn.**

Assembly Illustration

decreases increases decreases increases

Rnd 2: Ch 2 *(counts as first hdc)*, hdc in each st around with 2 hdc in each corner, join with sl st in top of ch-2, **do not turn.**

Rnd 3: Ch 1, sl st in each st around, join with sl st in first sl st. Fasten off.♦

Colors of Fall Shawl

Designed by Melinda Wigington

Soft earth tones accented with rich autumn hues of gold and scarlet inspired the color palette of this rustic and smartly-styled shawl that's the perfect warm-up wrap for any casual outfit!

FINISHED SIZE: One size fits all.

MATERIALS: Worsted yarn—10 oz. each gold, taupe, tan and rust; H double-ended and H crochet hooks or hook sizes needed to obtain gauge.

GAUGE: With **double-ended hook,** 5 sts = 1"; 8 rows = 1".

NOTE: Read General Instructions on page 6 before beginning pattern.

CENTER BACK BLOCK

Row 1: With double-ended hook and taupe, ch 75, pull up lp in second ch from hook, pull up lp in each ch across, turn. *(75 lps on hook)*

Row 2: With rust, work lps off hook, **do not turn.**

Row 3: Ch 1, skip first vertical bar, pull up lp in top strand of each **horizontal bar** across *(see illustration),* turn.

Horizontal Bar

Row 4: With tan, work lps off hook, **do not turn.**

Row 5: Ch 1, skip first vertical bar, pull up lp in top strand of each horizontal bar across, turn.

Row 6: With gold, work lps off hook, **do not turn.**

Row 7: Ch 1, skip first vertical bar, pull up lp in top strand of each horizontal bar across, turn.

Row 8: With taupe, work lps off hook, **do not turn.**

Row 9: Ch 1, skip first vertical bar, pull up lp in top strand of each horizontal bar across, turn.

Rows 10-138: Repeat rows 2-9 consecutively, ending with row 2.

Row 139: Ch 1, skip first vertical bar, sl st in top strand of each horizontal bar across. Fasten off.

For **edging,** with predominantly taupe/tan side facing you, with H hook and rust, join with sl st in end of row 1 on lower right corner, (skip next row, sl st in end of next row) across. Fasten off.

SIDE PANEL (make 2)

Row 1: With double-ended hook and taupe, ch 100, pull up lp in second ch from hook, pull up lp in each ch across, turn. *(100 lps on hook)*

Rows 2-139: Repeat same rows of Center Back Block.

For **first Side Panel edging,** with predominantly taupe/tan side facing you, with H hook and rust, join with sl st in end of last row on upper left corner, (skip next row, sl st in end of next row) across. Fasten off.

Holding first Side Panel edging against edging on side of Center Back Block, matching sts, with rust, sew together *(see assembly illustration).*

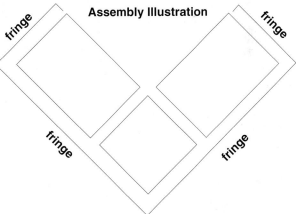

Assembly Illustration

For **second Side Panel edging,** with predominantly taupe/tan side facing you, with H hook and rust, join with sl st in end of first row on lower right corner, (skip next row, sl st in end of next row) across. Fasten off.

Holding second Side Panel edging against last row of Center Back Block, easing to fit, with rust, sew together.

continued on page 139

Faux Mink Wrap

DESIGNED BY CAROLYN CHRISTMAS

You'll love the luxurious look and feel of this heavenly wrap that's crocheted in silky-soft, thick chenille for a fashion accessory that's simply divine!

FINISHED SIZE: 12" x 52".

MATERIALS: 200 yds. brown thick chenille yarn; 3 oz. black worsted yarn; Crochenit™ hook.

GAUGE: 5 sts = 2"; 5 rows = 1".

NOTE: Read General Instructions and Crochenit™ Tips on page 8 before beginning pattern.

WRAP

Row 1: With chenille, ch 130, pull up lp in second ch from hook, pull up lp in each ch across, turn. *(130 lps on hook)*

Row 2: With worsted yarn, work lps off hook, **do not turn.**

Row 3: Skip first vertical bar, pull up lp in each vertical bar across, turn.

Row 4: With chenille, work lps off hook, **do not turn.**

Row 5: Skip first vertical bar, pull up lp in each vertical bar across, turn.

Rows 6-60: Repeat rows 2-5 consecutively, ending with row 4.

Row 61: Skip first vertical bar, sl st in each vertical bar across. Fasten off.♦

Colors of Fall Shawl

continued from page 137

FRINGE

For **each Fringe,** cut 4 strands each color each 36" long. Holding all strands together, insert one end of strands through st or row, pull ends even. Separate strands into two sections of four strands of each color; tie in knot ½" from top of strands.

Fringe in every third row or st around outer edge of Shawl as shown in illustration. With one strand of each color in each section, tie a second and third row of knots 1¼" below first row of knots according to Fringe illustration.♦

Knotted Fringe

First row of knots

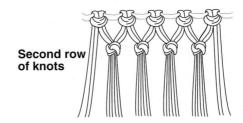

Second row of knots

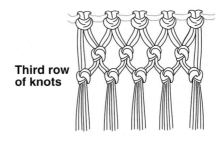

Third row of knots

Killarny Scalloped Stole

Designed by Joyce Nordstrom

A large-size hook and cozy, worsted yarn create this softly-textured shoulder warmer that's worked in one easy piece from beginning to end.

FINISHED SIZE: 24" wide x 70" long.

MATERIALS: 11 oz. each of aran and flecked worsted yarn; J double-ended hook.

GAUGE: 7 sts = 2".

SPECIAL STITCHES: For **open sc lp,** yo, skip next vertical bar, pull up lp in next vertical bar, yo, pull through one lp on hook.

For **4 sts decrease (4 st dec),** (skip next vertical bar, pull up lp in next vertical bar) 2 times, yo, pull through 2 lps on hook, yo, pull through one lp on hook.

For **double decrease (dbl dec),** yo, (skip next vertical bar, pull up lp in next vertical bar) 3 times, yo, pull through 3 lps on hook, yo, pull through one lp on hook.

NOTES: Read General Instructions on page 6 before beginning pattern.

STOLE

Row 1: With aran, ch 109, pull up lp in second ch from hook, pull up lp in each ch across, turn. *(109 lps on hook)*

Row 2: With flecked, work lps off hook, **do not turn.**

Row 3: Ch 1, skip first vertical bar *(see illustration),* yo, (skip next vertical bar, pull up lp in next vertical bar) 2 times, yo, pull through 2 lps on hook, yo, pull through one lp on hook *(dec made),* *◊(yo, skip next vertical bar, pull up lp in next vertical bar) 4 times, (yo, pull up lp in next vertical bar) 4 times, (yo, skip next vertical bar, pull up lp next vertical bar) 4 times◊, yo, (skip next vertical bar, pull up lp in next vertical bar) 3 times, yo, pull through 3 lps on hook, yo, pull through one lp on hook *(dec made);* repeat from * 2 more times; repeat between ◊◊, yo, (skip next vertical bar, pull up lp in next vertical bar) 2 times, yo, pull through 2 lps on hook, yo, pull through one lp on hook, yo, skip next vertical bar, pull up lp in last vertical bar, turn.

Row 4: With aran, work lps off hook, **do not turn.**

Row 5: Ch 1, skip first vertical bar, pull up lp in each vertical bar and in each lp across, turn. *(109 lps on hook)*

Rows 6-14: Repeat rows 2-5 consecutively, ending with row 2.

Row 15: Ch 1, skip first vertical bar, yo, **4 st dec** *(see Special Stitches),* *◊**open sc lp** *(see Special Stitches)* 4 times, (yo, pull up lp in next vertical bar) 4 times, open sc lp 4 times◊, **dbl dec** *(see Special Stitches);* repeat from * 2 more times; repeat between ◊◊, yo, 4 st dec, yo, skip next vertical bar, pull up lp in last vertical bar, turn.

Row 16: With aran, work lps off hook, **do not turn.**

Row 17: Ch 1, skip first vertical bar, yo, 4 st dec, *◊open sc lp 4 times, (yo, pull up lp in next vertical bar) 4 times, open sc lp 4 times◊, dbl dec; repeat from * 2 more times; repeat between ◊◊, yo, 4 st dec, yo, skip next vertical bar, pull up lp in last vertical bar, turn.

Row 18: With flecked, work lps off hook, **do not turn.**

Rows 19-196: Repeat rows 15-18 consecutively, ending with row 16 and aran.

Row 197: Ch 1, skip first vertical bar, pull up lp in each vertical bar across, turn *(109 lps on hook)*

Row 198: With flecked, work lps off hook, **do not turn.**

Row 199: Ch 1, skip first vertical bar, yo, (skip next vertical bar, pull up lp in next vertical bar) 2 times, yo, pull through 2 lps on hook, yo, pull through one lp on hook *(dec made),* *◊(yo, skip next vertical bar, pull up lp in next vertical bar) 4 times, (yo, pull up lp in next vertical bar) 4 times, (yo, skip next vertical bar, pull up lp next vertical bar) 4 times◊, yo, (skip next vertical bar, pull up lp in next vertical bar) 3 times, yo, pull through 3 lps on hook, yo, pull through one lp on hook *(dec made);* repeat from * 2 more times; repeat be-
continued on page 143

Classic Man's Scarf

DESIGNED BY CAROLYN CHRISTMAS

Bulky yarn worked in a distinctively masculine and ruggedly handsome striped pattern makes this smartly-styled scarf the perfect winter warmer for all the men on your holiday gift list!

SIZE: 8½" wide x 51½" long.

MATERIALS: Bulky yarn—5 oz. each off-white and green; Crochenit™ hook.

GAUGE: 2 corn sts = 2½", 3 basic sts = 1½"; 2 shell rows, 2 corn sts rows = 2"; 5 basic rows 1¼".

CROCHENIT™ STITCHES: Basic Stitch # 101; Corn Stitch #305.

SPECIAL STITCH: For **corn stitch (corn st),** pull up lp in first ch of next ch-3, insert hook under top strand of 2 horizontal bars above next shell 3 rows below, yo, pull lp through, ch 1, pull up lp in last ch of same ch-3.

NOTE: Read General Instructions on page 8 before beginning pattern.

SCARF

Row 1: With green, ch 126, pull up lp in second ch from hook, pull up lp in each ch across, turn. *(126 lps on hook)*

Row 2: With off-white, work lps off hook, **do not turn.**

Row 3: Skip first vertical bar, pull up lp in each vertical bar across, turn.

Row 4: With green, work lps off hook, **do not turn.**

Row 5: Skip first vertical bar, pull up lp in each vertical bar across, turn.

Row 6: With off-white, work first 3 lps off hook, yo, pull through 4 lps on hook *(shell made),* *ch 2, yo, pull through 4 lps on hook *(ch-3 and shell made)*; repeat from * 38 more times, work remaining lps off hook, **do not turn.**

Row 7: Skip first vertical bar, pull up lp in next 2 vertical bars, *skip next shell, pull up lp in first ch of next ch-3, insert hook in ch directly below on row 1, yo, pull lp through, ch 1, pull up lp in last ch of same ch-3 sp *(this completes a corn st)*; repeat from * 38 more times, skip next shell, pull up lp in last 3 vertical bars, turn.

Row 8: With green, work first 3 lps off hook, (ch 2, yo, pull through 4 lps on hook) 39 times, ch 2, work remaining lps off hook, **do not turn.**

Row 9: Skip first vertical bar, pull up lp in next 2 vertical bars, **corn st** *(see Special Stitch),* (skip next shell, corn st) 39 times, pull up lp in last 3 vertical bars, turn. *(126 lps on hook)*

Row 10: With off-white, work first 3 lps off hook, yo, pull through 4 lps on hook, *ch 2, yo, pull through 4 lps on hook *(ch-3 and shell made)*; repeat from * 38 more times, work remaining lps off hook, **do not turn.**

Row 11: Skip first vertical bar, pull up lp in first 2 vertical bars, (skip next shell, corn st) 39 times, skip next shell, pull up lp in last 3 vertical bars, turn. *(123 lps on hook)*

Rows 12-29: Repeat rows 8-11 consecutively, ending with row 9.

Rows 30-34: Repeat rows 2-4.

Row 35: Skip first vertical bar, sl st in each vertical bar across. Fasten off.♦

Killarny Scalloped Stole

continued from page 141

tween ◊◊, yo, (skip next vertical bar, pull up lp in next vertical bar) 2 times, yo, pull through 2 lps on hook, yo, pull through one lp on hook, yo, skip next vertical bar, pull up lp in last vertical bar, turn.

Row 200: With aran, work lps off hook, **do not turn.**

Row 201: Ch 1, skip first vertical bar, pull up lp in each vertical bar across, turn.

Rows 202-208: Repeat rows 198-201 consecutively, ending with row 200.

Row 209: Ch 1, sl st in each vertical bar across. Fasten off.♦

Christmas
Creations

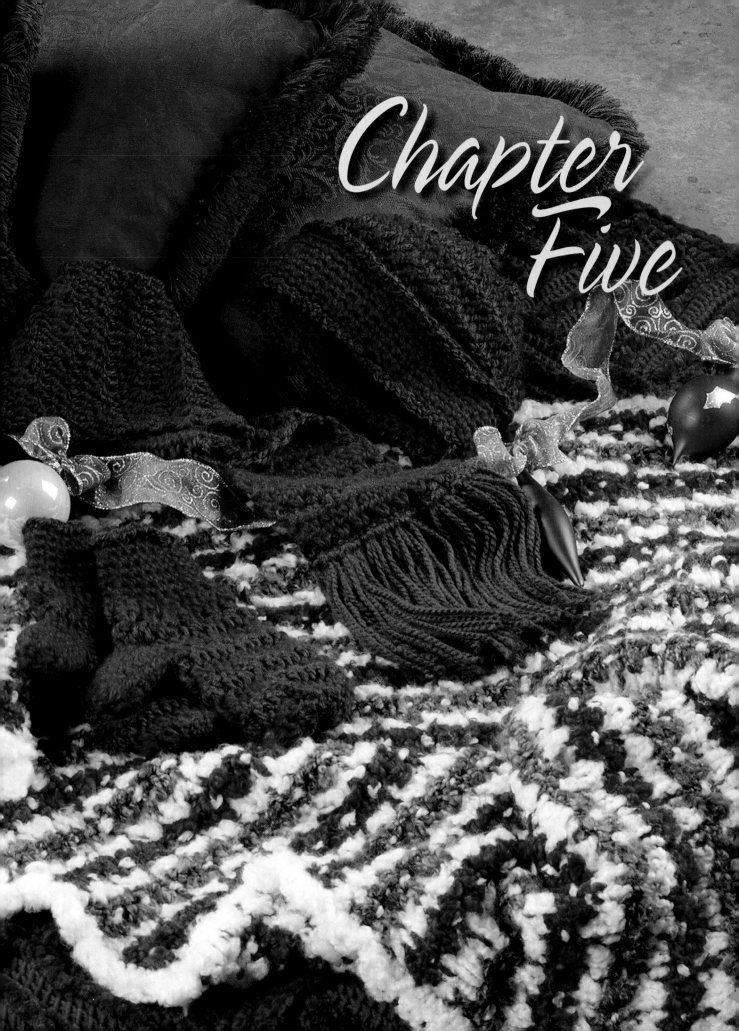

Chapter
Five

Cozy Christmas

DESIGNED BY MELINDA WIGINGTON

Bold stripes of peppermint colors create the delectable design in this holiday afghan and pillow set that works up fast in bulky weight yarn on an extra-large-size hook.

Afghan

FINISHED SIZE: 36½" x 48".

MATERIALS: Bulky yarn—27 oz. white, 12 oz. each burgundy and green; Q double-ended hook or hook size needed to obtain gauge.

GAUGE: 3 shells and 3 sts = 4"; 7 rows = 3".

SPECIAL STITCH: For **shell,** yo, pull through 4 lps on hook.

NOTE: Read General Instructions on page 6 before beginning pattern.

AFGHAN

Row 1: With white, ch 109, pull up lp in second ch from hook, pull up lp in each ch across, turn. *(109 lps on hook)*

Row 2: With burgundy, pull through first lp on hook, **shell** *(see Special Stitch),* yo, pull through 2 lps on hook, (shell, yo, pull through 2 lps on hook) across, **do not turn.**

Row 3: Skip first vertical bar, *pull up lp in top strand of next **horizontal bar** *(see illustration),* pull up lp in top of next shell, pull up lp in top strand of next horizontal bar, pull up lp in next vertical bar; repeat from * across, turn. *(109 lps on hook)*

Horizontal Bar

Rows 4-108: Working in color sequence of white, green, white and burgundy, repeat rows 2 and 3 alternately, ending with row 2 and white.

Row 109: Ch 1, sc in first vertical bar, skip next horizontal bar, 3 sc in top of next shell, skip next horizontal bar, (sl st in next vertical bar, skip next horizontal bar, 3 sc in top of next shell, skip

next horizontal bar) across to last vertical bar, sc in last vertical bar. Fasten off.

For **first side edging,** working in ends of rows, join white with sc in last row, 2 sc in same sp, (skip next row, sl st in next row, skip next row, 3 sc in next row) across. Fasten off.

For **second side edging,** working in ends of rows on other side, join white with sc in row 1, 2 sc in same sp, (skip next row, sl st in next row, skip next row, 3 sc in next row) across. Fasten off.

Pillow

SIZE: 18" x 21".

MATERIALS: Bulky yarn—5 oz. each white, burgundy and green; 14" x 17" pillow form; tapestry needle; P double-ended hook or hook size needed to obtain gauge.

GAUGE: 3 sts = 2"; 6 rows = 2".

NOTE: Read General Instructions on page 6 before beginning pattern.

PILLOW SIDE (make 2)

Row 1: With burgundy, ch 21, pull up lp in second ch from hook, pull up lp in each ch across, turn. *(21 lps on hook)*

Row 2: With green, work loops off hook, **do not turn.**

Row 3: Skip first vertical bar, pull up lp in each vertical bar across, turn.

Row 4: With burgundy, work lps off hook, **do not turn.**

Row 5: Skip first vertical bar, pull up lp in each vertical bar across, turn.

Rows 6-50: Repeat rows 2-5 consecutively, ending with row 2.

Row 51: Skip first vertical bar, sl st in each vertical bar across. Fasten off.

For **border,** working around outer edge, join white with sc in first st of last row, 2 sc in same st, sc in each st across to last st, 3 sc in last st, evenly space 30 sc across ends of rows; working in

continued on page 153

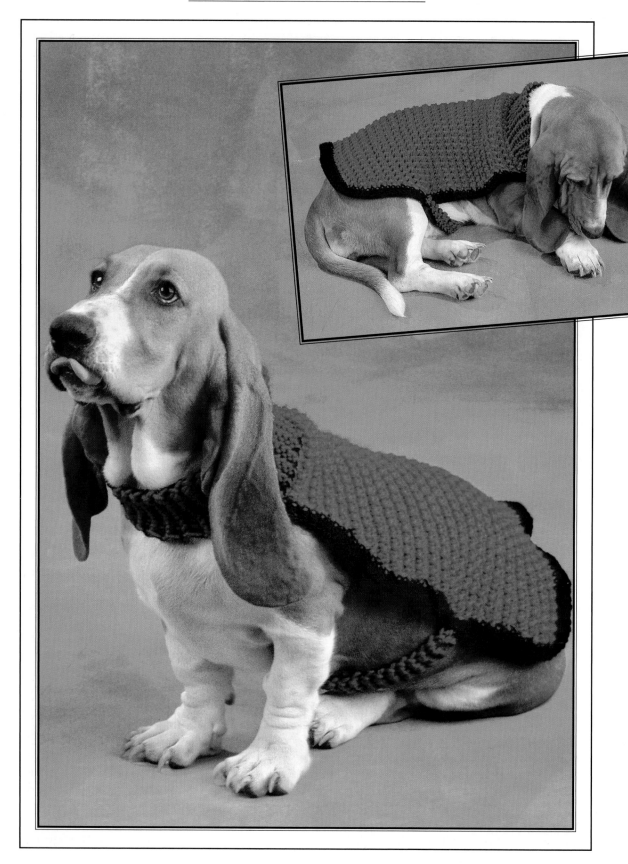

Santa's Little Helper Sweater

DESIGNED BY DEBBIE TABOR

Everyone needs a fancy outfit for the holidays, even the family's best friend! Made in colorful worsted yarn with a large hook, you can easily adapt this festive sweater to fit smaller or larger dogs simply by changing hook sizes.

FINISHED SIZE: 13" wide and 19" long.

MATERIALS: Worsted yarn—3 oz. each red and burgundy, 2½ oz. black; ¾" side release buckle; stitch markers; tapestry needle; J double-ended and G crochet hooks or hook sizes needed to obtain gauges.

GAUGES: With **double-ended hook,** 5 cr sts = 2"; 6 rows = 1". With **G hook,** 4 sts =1".

SPECIAL STITCH: For **cross stitch (cr st),** skip next vertical bar, pull up lp in next vertical bar; working in front of last st, pull up lp in skipped vertical bar.

NOTE: Read General Instructions on page 6 before beginning pattern.

SWEATER

Row 1: Starting at **front,** with double-ended hook and red, ch 47, pull up lp in second ch from hook, pull up lp in each ch across, turn. *(47 lps on hook)*

Row 2: With burgundy, work lps off hook, **do not turn.**

Row 3: Skip first vertical bar, **cr st** *(see Special Stitch)* across, turn.

Row 4: With red, work lps off hook, **do not turn.**

Row 5: Skip first vertical bar, pull up lp in top strand of each **horizontal bar** across *(see illustration),* turn.

Rows 6-16: Repeat rows 2-5 consecutively, ending with row 4.

Row 17: Pull up lp in first vertical bar, (pull up lp in top strand of next horizontal bar, pull up lp in next ver-

Horizontal Bar

tical bar) 2 times, pull up lp in top strand of each horizontal bar across to last 3 vertical bars, pull up lp in next vertical bar, (pull up lp in top strand of next horizontal bar, pull up lp in next vertical bar) 2 times, turn. *(53 lps on hook)*

Rows 18-24: Repeat rows 2-5 consecutively, ending with row 4.

Row 25: Repeat row 17. *(59 lps on hook)*

Rows 26-87: Repeat rows 2-5 consecutively, ending with row 3.

Row 88: With red, pull through first 2 lps on hook, yo, pull through 3 lps on hook, (yo, pull through 2 lps on hook) across to last 5 lps on hook, (yo, pull through 3 lps on hook) 2 times, **do not turn.**

Row 89: Skip first vertical bar, pull up lp in top strand of each horizontal bar across, turn. *(55 lps on hook)*

Row 90: With burgundy, work lps off hook, **do not turn.**

Row 91: Repeat row 3.

Row 92: With red, work lps off hook, **do not turn.**

Row 93: Sl st in top strand of each horizontal bar across. Fasten off.

COLLAR

Row 1: With double-ended hook and black, ch 10, pull up lp in second ch from hook, pull up lp in each ch across, turn. *(10 lps on hook)*

Row 2: With burgundy, work lps off hook, **do not turn.**

Row 3: Skip first vertical bar, pull up lp under each horizontal bar across, turn.

Row 4: With black, work lps off hook, **do not turn.**

Row 5: Skip first vertical bar, pull up lp under each horizontal bar across, turn.

Rows 6-140 or to desired length to fit comfortably around dog's neck: Repeat rows 2-5

continued on page 153

Puppy and Kitty Christmas Stockings

Designed by Sue Penrod

Santa will be sure not to forget our furry, four-legged family members when he sees these adorable stockings hung with care and ready to be filled with tempting treats and toys!

PUPPY

FINISHED SIZE: 13" long not including hanging loop.

MATERIALS: Worsted yarn—5 oz. each brown and tan, small amount each black, red and white; tapestry needle; J double-ended crochet hook or hook size needed to obtain gauge.

GAUGE: 4 sts = 1"; 6 rows = 1".

NOTE: Read General Instructions on page 6 before beginning pattern.

STOCKING

Row 1: Starting at **top,** with brown, ch 60, pull up lp in second ch from hook, pull up lp in next 24 chs; for **hanging loop,** skip next 10 chs; draw up lp in last 25 chs, turn. *(50 lps on hook)*

Row 2: With tan, work lps off hook, **do not turn.**

Row 3: Skip first vertical bar, pull up lp in top strand of each **horizontal bar** across *(see illustration)* turn.

Horizontal Bar

Row 4: With brown, work lps off hook, **do not turn.**

Row 5: Skip first vertical bar, pull up lp in top strand of each horizontal bar across, turn.

Rows 6-48: Repeat rows 2-5 consecutively, ending with row 4.

Row 49: Ch 6, pull up lp in second ch from hook, pull up lp in next 4 chs, pull up lp in top strand of each horizontal bar across, turn. *(56 lps on hook)*

Row 50: With tan, work lps off hook, **do not turn.**

Row 51: Repeat row 49. *(62 lps on hook)*

Row 52: With brown, work lps off hook, **do**

not turn.

Row 53: Skip first vertical bar, pull up lp in top strand of each horizontal bar across, turn.

Rows 54-60: Repeat rows 2-5 consecutively, ending with row 4.

Row 61: Repeat row 49. *(68 lps on hook)*

Row 62: With tan, work lps off hook, **do not turn.**

Row 63: Repeat row 49. *(74 lps on hook)*

Row 64: With brown, work lps off hook, **do not turn.**

Row 65: Skip first vertical bar, pull up lp in top strand of each horizontal bar across, turn.

Rows 66-80: Repeat rows 2-5 consecutively, ending with row 4.

Row 81: Skip first vertical bar, sl st in top strand of each horizontal bar across. Leaving long end for sewing, fasten off.

Fold Stocking in half lengthwise, matching sts and ends of rows, sew together across bottom and front side leaving top open.

EAR (make 2)

Row 1: With brown, ch 10, pull up lp in second ch from hook, pull up lp in each ch across, turn. *(10 lps on hook)*

Row 2: With tan, work lps off hook, **do not turn.**

Row 3: Skip first vertical bar, pull up lp in top strand of each horizontal bar across, turn.

Row 4: With brown, work lps off hook, **do not turn.**

Row 5: Skip first vertical bar, pull up lp in top strand of each horizontal bar across, turn.

Rows 6-12: Repeat rows 2-5 consecutively, ending with row 4.

Row 13: Skip first vertical bar, sl st in top strand of each horizontal bar across, **do not turn.**

Row 14: Working in ends of rows, ch 1, pull up lp in every other row across, yo, pull through all lps on hook to gather end of Ear. Leaving long end for sewing, fasten off.

Sew gathered end of Ears over rows 48-50 at an angle on each side of Stocking as shown in photo.

For **nose,** with black, ch 2, (sc, hdc, dc, tr, dc, hdc, sc) in second ch from hook. Fasten off. Sew over rows 60-62 on corner of Stocking as shown.

For **tongue,** with red, ch 3, (4 dc, hdc, sl st) in third ch from hook. Fasten off. Tuck bottom corner of Stocking to the inside; tack in place sewing tongue inside tuck as shown.

For **eyes,** embroider one black French knot *(see illustration)* over rows 53-55 on each side of Stocking.

For **eyebrows,** embroider one black straight stitch *(see illustration)* at an angle above each French knot.

French Knot

For **eye sparkles,** with white, embroider one small straight stitch to bottom of each French knot.

With straight stitch, embroider black **nose and mouthlines** centered under nose over seam and working across in a curve on each side as shown in photo.

Straight Stitch

KITTEN

FINISHED SIZE: 12½" long not including hanging loop.

MATERIALS: Worsted yarn—5 oz. gray with black and white flecks, small amount each black and pink; 5 oz. white bulky yarn; tapestry needle; J double-ended crochet hook or hook size needed to obtain gauge.

GAUGE: 3 sts = 1"; 4 rows = 1".

NOTE: Read General Instructions on page 6 before beginning pattern.

SPECIAL STITCH: For **double crochet loop (dc lp),** yo, pull up lp in next vertical bar, yo, pull through 2 lps on hook.

STOCKING

Row 1: Starting at **top,** with white, ch 40, pull up lp in second ch from hook, pull up lp in each ch across, turn. *(40 lps on hook)*

Row 2: With gray, work lps off hook, **do not turn.**

Row 3: Ch 1, skip first vertical bar, **dc lp** *(see Special Stitch)* in each vertical bar across, turn.

Row 4: With white, work lps off hook, **do not turn.**

Row 5: Ch 1, skip first vertical bar, pull up lp in each vertical bar across, turn.

Rows 6-32: Repeat rows 2-5 consecutively, ending with row 4.

Row 33: Ch 1, skip first vertical bar, pull up lp in next 14 vertical bars, (pull up lp in top strand of next **horizontal bar**—*see illustration on page 151,* pull up lp in next vertical bar) 10 times, pull up lp in last 15 vertical bars, turn. *(50 lps on hook)*

Rows 34-48: Repeat rows 2-5 consecutively, ending with row 4.

Row 49: Ch 1, skip first vertical bar, pull up lp in next 14 vertical bars, (insert hook through next 2 vertical bars at same time, yo, pull up lp) 10 times, pull up lp in last 15 vertical bars, turn. *(40 lps on hook)*

Row 50: With gray, work lps off hook, **do not turn.**

Row 51: Sl st in each vertical bar across. Leaving long end for sewing, fasten off.

Fold Stocking in half lengthwise, matching sts and ends of rows, sew together across bottom and long straight edge leaving top open.

For **hanger,** join white with sl st in seam at top of Stocking, ch 10, sl st in same sp. Fasten off.

MUZZLE

Row 1: With white, ch 4, pull up lp in second ch from hook, pull up lp in each ch across, turn. *(4 lps on hook)*

Row 2: With gray, work lps off hook, **do not turn.**

Row 3: Skip first vertical bar, pull up lp under both strands of each horizontal bar across, turn.

Row 4: With white, work lps off hook, **do not turn.**

Row 5: Skip first vertical bar, pull up lp under both strands of each horizontal bar across, turn.

Rows 6-36: Repeat rows 2-5 consecutively, ending with row 4. At end of last row, fasten off.

Fold Muzzle into a semi-circle and sew to front of Stocking over rows 39-46 as shown in photo.

For **nose,** with pink, ch 3, (sc, hdc, dc, hdc, sc) in third ch from hook. Fasten off. Sew to center of Muzzle.

With pink, using straight stitch, embroider **nose and mouthlines** starting at center bottom of nose and around curve of Muzzle.

For **whisker,** cut one 2" piece black yarn. Fold in half, insert hook in Muzzle on one side of nose, pull fold through, pull both loose ends through fold, tighten. Unravel yarn. Repeat on other side of nose.

EAR (make 2)
Row 1: With white, ch 5, sc in second ch from hook, sc in each ch across, turn. *(4 sc made)*

Row 2: Ch 1, sc in first 3 sts leaving last st unworked, turn. *(3) Unworked st will be top point of Ear.*

Row 3: Ch 1, skip first st, sc in last 2 sts. Fasten off. Tack end of first and last row together on bottom of Ear.

Sew at an angle over rows 35-38 on each side of Stocking as shown.

With black, using fly stitch *(see illustration),* embroider **eyes** to Stocking above Muzzle.♦

Fly Stitch

Cozy Christmas
continued from page 147

starting ch on opposite side of row 1, 3 sc in first ch, sc in each ch across to last ch, 3 sc in last ch, evenly space 30 sc across ends of rows, join with sl st in first sc. Fasten off.

RUFFLE
Rnd 1: To join, holding both Sides with predominantly burgundy side and predominantly green side facing each other, working through both thicknesses, matching sts, join white with sc in any center corner st, sc in same st, sc in each st around with 3 sc in each center corner st inserting pillow form before closing, sc in same st as first sc, join with sl st in first sc.

Rnd 2: Ch 3 *(counts as first dc),* 2 dc in same st, sc in next st, (3 dc in next st, sc in next st) around, join with sl st in top of ch-3. Fasten off.♦

Santa's Little Helper Sweater
continued from page 149

consecutively, ending with row 4.

Row 141: Sl st under each horizontal bar across. Fasten off.

Sew first and last rows together. Easing to fit, sew one side of Collar to starting ch on opposite side of row 1 on Sweater.

EDGING
Row 1: Working in ends of rows and in sts on Sweater, with predominantly red side facing you, with G hook and black, join with sc in first row after Collar, evenly spacing sts so piece lays flat, sc across to row 1 on other side of Sweater, turn.

Row 2: Ch 3 *(counts as first dc),* dc in each st across, sl st in next st on Sweater. Fasten off.

STRAP (make 2)
Row 1: With double-ended hook and black, ch 4, pull up lp in second ch from hook, pull up lp in each ch across, turn. *(4 lps on hook)*

Row 2: With burgundy, work lps off hook, **do not turn.**

Row 3: Skip first vertical bar, pull up lp under each horizontal bar across, turn.

Row 4: With black, work lps off hook, **do not turn.**

Row 5: Skip first vertical bar, pull up lp under each horizontal bar across, turn.

Rows 6-64: Repeat rows 2-5 consecutively, ending with row 4.

Row 65: Sl st in top strand of each horizontal bar across. Fasten off.

Sew buckle pieces to one end of each Strap. Try Sweater on dog; place stitch markers in ends of row near dog's tummy. Remove Sweater. Sew Strap ends to marked row.♦

Yuletide Helpers

Designed by Susie Spier Maxfield

Serve your yuletide goodies in festive style on holiday place mats and hot pads that work up quickly in easy-care worsted cotton yarn. A matching dishcloth makes cleanup a snap!

FINISHED SIZE: Hot Pad and Dishcloth are 7½" x 8" each. Place Mat is 13" x 19".

MATERIALS FOR ONE SET: 100% cotton 4-ply yarn—8 oz. red and 6 oz. white; J double-ended and H crochet hooks or hook sizes needed to obtain gauges.

GAUGES: With **double-ended hook,** 3 pattern sts = 2"; 5 rows = 1". With **H hook,** 2 shells and 2 sc worked in Border = 2".

NOTE: Read General Instructions on page 6 before beginning pattern.

HOT PAD
Side (make 2)
Row 1: With double-ended hook and red, ch 29, pull up lp in second ch from hook, pull up lp in each ch across, turn. *(29 lps on hook)*

Row 2: With white, work lps off hook, **do not turn.**

Row 3: Ch 1, skip first vertical bar, *yo, pull up lp in top strand of next 3 **horizontal bars** *(see illustration),* pick up first lp of 3-lp group and bring off hook over last 2 lps; repeat from * across to last horizontal bar, pull up lp in top strand of last horizontal bar, turn. *(9 pattern sts)*

Horizontal Bar

Row 4: With red, work lps off hook, **do not turn.**

Row 5: Ch 1, skip first vertical bar, (yo, pull up lp in top strand of next 3 horizontal bars, pick up first lp of 3-lp group and bring off hook over last 2 lps) across to last horizontal bar, pull up lp in top strand of last horizontal bar, turn.

Rows 6-32: Repeat rows 2-5 consecutively, ending with row 4.

Row 33: Ch 1, sl st in top strand of each horizontal bar across. Fasten off.

Border
Rnd 1: Holding Sides wrong sides together, working through both thicknesses, with H hook and red, join with sc in first st of last row, (skip next st, sc in next st) across to next corner, ch 1; working in ends of rows, evenly space 19 sc across, ch 1; working in starting ch on opposite side of row 1, sc in first ch, (skip next ch, sc in next ch) across to next corner, ch 1; working in ends of rows, evenly space 19 sc across, ch 1, join with sl st in first sc, **turn,** sl st in ch sp just made, **turn.** *(15 sc across each short end between corner ch-1 sps, 19 sc across each long side between corner ch-1 sps)*

Rnd 2: Ch 1, sc in same ch sp, skip next st, 5 dc in next st, skip next st; working in sts and corner ch sps, (sc in next st, skip next st, 5 dc in next st, skip next st) around, join. Fasten off.

DISHCLOTH
Work same as Hot Pad Side, making only one piece.

Border
Work same as Hot Pad Border, working around one thickness of Dishcloth only.

PLACE MAT
Row 1: With double-ended hook and red, ch 80, pull up lp in second ch from hook, pull up lp in each ch across, turn. *(80 lps on hook)*

Row 2: With white, work lps off hook, **do not turn.**

Row 3: Ch 1, skip first vertical bar, (yo, pull up lp in top strand of next 3 horizontal bars, pick up first lp of 3-lp group bring off hook over last 2 lps) across to last horizontal bar, pull up lp in top strand of last horizontal bar, turn. *(26 pattern sts)*

continued on page 157

Ribbed Chenille Afghan

DESIGNED BY NANCY NEHRING

Richly textured blocks of dimensional ribbing are alternately arranged in horizontal and vertical patterns to create the eye-catching design in this luscious throw. It works up smoothly and easily in fleecy-soft, bulky weight chenille with a large-size hook.

FINISHED SIZE: 52" square.

MATERIALS: 28 oz. red worsted yarn; 700 yds. burgundy thick chenille yarn; tapestry needle; K double-ended and K crochet hooks or hook sizes needed to obtain gauges.

GAUGES: With **double-ended hook,** 3 sts = 1"; rows 4-11 = 2". With **K hook and chenille yarn,** 3 sc = 2". Each Block is 7" square.

NOTE: Read General Instructions on page 6 before beginning pattern.

BLOCK (make 49)

Row 1: With double-ended hook and worsted yarn, ch 22, pull up lp in **back lp** *(see Stitch Guide)* of second ch from hook, pull up lp in **back lp** of each ch across, turn. *(22 lps on hook)*

Row 2: With chenille yarn, work lps off hook, **do not turn.**

Row 3: Ch 1, pull up lp under first **horizontal bar** *(see illustration),* pull up lp under each horizontal bar across, turn.

Row 4: With worsted yarn, work lps off hook, **do not turn.**

Row 5: Skip first vertical bar, pull up lp in each vertical bar across, **do not turn.**

Rows 6-9: Repeat rows 4 and 5 alternately. At end of last row, turn.

Rows 10-36: Repeat rows 2-9 consecutively, ending with row 4.

Row 37: Skip first vertical bar, sl st in each vertical bar across. Fasten off.

Holding Blocks wrong sides together, with worsted yarn, sew together in seven rows of seven Blocks each with "ribs" alternating vertically and horizontally.

BORDER

Rnd 1: Working in sts and in ends of rows around entire outer edge, with K hook and chenille yarn, join with sc in any st, evenly spacing sts so piece lays flat, sc around with 3 sc in each corner, join with sl st in first sc.

Rnd 2: Ch 1, sc in each st around with 3 sc in each center corner st, join. Fasten off.♦

Horizontal Bar

Yuletide Helpers

continued from page 155
continued from page 155

Row 4: With red, work lps off hook, **do not turn.**

Row 5: Ch 1, skip first vertical bar, (yo, pull up lp in top strand of next 3 horizontal bars, pick up first lp of 3-lp group and bring off hook over last 2 lps) across to last horizontal bar, pull up lp in top strand of last horizontal bar, turn.

Rows 6-56: Repeat rows 2-5 consecutively, ending with row 4.

Row 57: Ch 1, sl st in top strand of each horizontal bar across. Fasten off.

Border

Rnd 1: Working in rnds, with H hook and red, join with sc in first st of last row, sc in same st, (skip next st, sc in next st) across to last st, 3 sc in last st; working in ends of rows, evenly space 27 sc across; working in starting ch on opposite side of row 1, 3 sc in first ch, (skip next ch, sc in next ch) across to next last ch, 3 sc in last ch; working in ends of rows, evenly space 27 sc across, sc in same st as first sc, join with sl st in first sc, **turn.** *(144 sc)*

Rnd 2: Ch 1, sc in same st, skip next st, 5 dc in next st, skip next st, (sc in next st, skip next st, 5 dc in next st, skip next st) around, join. Fasten off.♦

Scarf, Hat & Mittens

DESIGNED BY TAMMY HILDEBRAND

What's more fun after a fresh, new snowfall than to have a good old-fashioned snowball fight? But first be sure to crochet this cuddly-soft winter warmer set to keep the frosty cold away!

FINISHED SIZES: Scarf is 6" wide. Hat fits adult-size head. Mittens are 7" long. Changes for 8" and 9" long are in [ ].

MATERIALS FOR ONE SET: Worsted yarn—4 [4½, 5] oz. each maroon and green; tapestry needle; K double-ended and K crochet hooks or hook sizes needed to obtain gauges.

GAUGES: With **double-ended hook,** 10 dc lps = 3"; 8 rows = 3". With **K hook,** 5 sc = 2".

SPECIAL STITCH: For **double crochet loop (dc lp),** yo, pull up lp in next vertical bar, yo, pull through 2 lps on hook.

NOTE: Read General Instructions on page 6 before beginning pattern.

SCARF

Row 1: With double-ended hook and green, ch 20, pull up lp in second ch from hook, pull up lp in each ch across, turn. *(20 lps on hook)*

Row 2: With maroon, pull through first lp on hook, (yo, pull through 2 lps on hook) across, **do not turn.**

Row 3: Ch 2, skip first vertical bar, **dc lp** *(see Special Stitch)* in top strand of each **horizontal bar** across *(see illustration),* turn.

Horizontal Bar

Row 4: With green, pull through first lp on hook, ch 1, yo, pull through 3 lps on hook, (ch 2, yo, pull through 3 lps on hook) across to last 2 lps on hook, ch 1, yo, pull through last 2 lps on hook, **do not turn.**

Row 5: Skip first vertical bar, pull up lp in each ch across to last vertical bar, pull up lp in last vertical bar, turn. *(20 lps on hook)*

Rows 6-140 or to desired length: Repeat rows 2-5 consecutively, ending with row 4.

Row 141: Ch 1, skip first vertical bar, sc in each ch across to last vertical bar, sc in last vertical bar. Fasten off.

Row 142: Working in starting ch on opposite side of row 1, join green with sc in first ch, sc in each ch across. Fasten off.

For **each fringe,** cut 3 strands green each 16" long. Holding all strands together, fold in half, insert hook in st, pull fold through, pull all loose ends through fold, tighten. Trim ends.

Make one fringe in each st across short ends of Scarf.

HAT

Row 1: With double-ended hook and maroon, ch 55, dc lp in third ch from hook, dc lp in each ch across, turn. *(54 dc lps made)*

Row 2: With green, pull through first lp on hook, ch 1, yo, pull through 3 lps on hook, (ch 2, yo, pull through 3 lps on hook) across to last 2 lps on hook, ch 1, yo, pull through last 2 lps on hook, **do not turn.**

Row 3: Skip first vertical bar, pull up lp in each ch across to last vertical bar, pull up lp in last vertical bar, turn.

Row 4: With maroon, pull through first lp on hook, (yo, pull through 2 lps on hook) across, **do not turn.**

Row 5: Ch 2, skip first vertical bar, dc lp in top strand of each horizontal bar across, turn.

Rows 6-27: Repeat rows 2-5 consecutively, ending with row 3. At end of last row, **do not turn,** with green, yo, pull through all lps on hook to gather, ch 1. Fasten off.

Matching row colors, sew ends of rows together.

continued on page 163

Christmas Ornaments

Designed by Lori Zeller

Quick as a wink with scraps of worsted yarn, you can stitch up a whole collection of festive ornaments to spruce up your tree or decorate your holiday packages!

Wreath
FINISHED SIZE: 3" x 3½" not including hanging loop.

MATERIALS: Sport yarn—small amount each dk. green and med. green; 8" green ¹⁄₁₆" satin ribbon; 9" red ¼" satin picot ribbon; 3 red 7mm rhinestones; 1¼" white silk poinsettia; craft glue or hot glue gun; tapestry needle; G double-ended crochet hook or hook size needed to obtain gauge.

GAUGE: 11 sts = 2"; 7 rows = 1".

NOTES: Read General Instructions on page 6 before beginning pattern.

WREATH
Row 1: With dk. green, ch 10, pull up lp in second ch from hook, pull up lp in each ch across, turn. *(10 lps on hook)*

Row 2: With med. green, work lps off hook, **do not turn.**

Row 3: Skip first vertical bar, pull up lp in top strand of each **horizontal bar** across *(see illustration),* turn.

Horizontal Bar

Row 4: With dk. green, work lps off hook, **do not turn.**

Row 5: Skip first vertical bar, pull up lp in top strand of each horizontal bar across, turn.

Rows 6-68: Repeat rows 2-5 consecutively, ending with row 4. At end of last row, leaving long end for sewing, fasten off.

Fold piece in half lengthwise, sew ends of rows together forming a long tube. Sew ends of tube together.

Tie red ribbon into a small bow and glue to center bottom of Wreath. Glue poinsettia over red bow. Glue rhinestones to wreath as desired.

For **hanging loop,** fold green ribbon in half.

Glue ends to top of Wreath on back side.

Tree
FINISHED SIZE: 3" x 4½" not including hanging loop.

MATERIALS: Sport yarn—small amount each dk. green and med. green; 8" green ¹⁄₁₆" satin ribbon; 7 red 7mm rhinestones; ½" angel charm; craft glue or hot glue gun; G double-ended and E crochet hooks or hook size needed to obtain gauge.

GAUGE: With **double-ended hook,** 11 sts = 2"; 7 rows = 1".

NOTES: Read General Instructions on page 6 before beginning pattern.

SIDE (make 2)
Row 1: With double-ended hook and dk. green, ch 2, pull up lp in second ch from hook, turn. *(2 lps on hook)*

Row 2: With med. green, work lps off hook, **do not turn.**

Row 3: Skip first vertical bar, pull up lp in top strand of next **horizontal bar** across *(see illustration),* pull up lp in last vertical bar, turn. *(3)*

Row 4: With dk. green, work lps off hook, **do not turn.**

Row 5: Skip first vertical bar, pull up lp in top strand of each horizontal bar across to last vertical bar, pull up lp in last vertical bar, turn. *(4)*

Row 6: With med. green, work lps off hook, **do not turn.**

Row 7: Skip first vertical bar, pull up lp in top strand of each horizontal bar across to last vertical bar, pull up lp in last vertical bar, turn. *(5)*

Row 8: With dk. green, work lps off hook, **do not turn.**

Rows 9-32: Repeat rows 5-8 consecutively, ending with *17 lps on hook* in row 31. At end of last row on first Side, fasten off. At end of last row on second Side, **do not fasten off.**

For **edging,** holding Sides wrong sides together,

matching sts and working through both thicknesses, with E hook, ch 1, skip first vertical bar, sc in top strand of next 8 horizontal bars, ch 2, sc in second ch from hook, sc around side of last sc made, sc in top strand of next 8 horizontal bars, ch 2, evenly space 15 sc across ends of rows, sc in ch on opposite side of row 1, ch 1, sl st in last sc made, sc in same ch, evenly space 15 sc across ends of rows, ch 2, join with sl st in first sc. Fasten off.

Glue angel charm to top point of Tree. Glue rhinestones to Tree as desired.

For **hanging loop,** fold green ribbon in half. Glue ends to top of Tree on back side.

Drums

FINISHED SIZES: Small Drum is 1½" tall not including hanging loop. Large Drum is 2" tall not including hanging loop.

MATERIALS FOR ONE OF EACH: Sport yarn—small amount each green, white and red; 1 yd. gold metallic size 5 crochet cotton thread; polyester fiberfill; tapestry needle; G double-ended and D crochet hooks or hook sizes needed to obtain gauges.

GAUGES: With **double-ended hook,** 11 sts = 2"; 7 rows = 1". With **D hook,** Small Drum's Top/Bottom is 1" across.

NOTES: Read General Instructions on page 6 before beginning pattern.

SMALL DRUM
Side

Row 1: With double-ended hook and green, ch 8, pull up lp in second ch from hook and in each ch across, turn. *(8 lps on hook)*

Row 2: With red, work lps off hook, **do not turn.**

Row 3: Skip first vertical bar, pull up lp in top strand of each **horizontal bar** across *(see illustration),* turn.

Row 4: With green, work lps off hook, **do not turn.**

Row 5: Skip first vertical bar, pull up lp in top strand of each horizontal bar across, turn.

Rows 6-28: Repeat rows 2-5 consecutively, ending with row 4. At end of last row, leaving long end for sewing, fasten off. Sew first and last rows together. *(Predominantly red side will be outside of Drum.)*

Top/Bottom (make 2)

Rnd 1: With D hook and white, ch 2, 7 sc in second ch from hook, join with sl st in first sc. *(7 sc made)*

Rnd 2: Ch 1, 2 sc in each st around, join. Fasten off.

Sew Top and Bottom pieces to ends of Drum through **back lps** only *(see Stitch Guide),* stuffing before closing.

With tapestry needle and gold crochet thread, embroider long zigzag sts around sides of Drum as shown in photo.

For **hanging loop,** tie desired length of gold crochet thread to st on one side of Drum.

LARGE DRUM
Side

Row 1: With double-ended hook and green, ch 11, pull up lp in second ch from hook and in each ch across, turn. *(11 lps on hook)*

Row 2: With red, work lps off hook, **do not turn.**

Row 3: Skip first vertical bar, pull up lp in top strand of each **horizontal bar** across *(see illustration),* turn.

Row 4: With green, work lps off hook, **do not turn.**

Row 5: Skip first vertical bar, pull up lp in top strand of each horizontal bar across, turn.

Rows 6-40: Repeat rows 2-5 consecutively, ending with row 4. At end of last row, leaving long end for sewing, fasten off. Sew first and last rows together. *(Predominantly green side will be outside of Drum.)*

Top/Bottom (make 2)

Rnds 1-2: Repeat same rnds of Small Drum's Top/Bottom. At end of last rnd, **do not fasten off.**

Rnd 3: Ch 1, sc in first st, 2 sc in next st, (sc in next st, 2 sc in next st) around, join. Fasten off.

Sew Top and Bottom pieces to ends of Drum through **back lps** only *(see Stitch Guide),* stuffing before closing.

With tapestry needle and gold crochet thread, embroider long zigzag sts around sides of Drum as shown in photo.

For **hanging loop,** tie desired length of gold crochet thread to st on one side of Drum.♦

Scarf, Hat & Mittens

continued from page 159

Brim

Rnd 1: Working in starting ch on opposite side of row 1, with right side of Hat facing you, with K hook and maroon, join with sc in first ch, sc in each ch around, join with sl st in first sc. *(54 sc made)*

Rnd 2: Ch 1, sc in each st around, join, **turn.**

Rnd 3: Working this rnd in **back lps** only *(see Stitch Guide on page 11),* ch 1, sc in each st around, join.

Rnds 4-9: Ch 1, sc in each st around, join. At end of last rnd, fasten off.

Rnd 10: With K hook and green, join with sl st in first st, ch 1, (sl st in next st, ch 1) around, join with sl st in first sl st. Fasten off.

For **trim,** with K hook and green, working in remaining lps of rnd 2, join with sl st in first st, ch 1, (sl st in next st, ch 1) around, join. Fasten off.

Fold Brim up over Hat.

MITTEN (make 2)

Row 1: With double-ended hook and maroon, ch 23 [25, 27], dc lp in third ch from hook, dc lp in each ch across, turn. *(22 dc lps made) [24 dc lps made, 26 dc lps made]*

Row 2: With green, pull through first lp on hook, ch 1, yo, pull through 3 lps on hook, (ch 2, yo, pull through 3 lps on hook) across to last 2 lps on hook, ch 1, yo, pull through last 2 lps on hook, **do not turn.**

Row 3: Skip first vertical bar, pull up lp in top strand of each ch across to last vertical bar, pull up lp in last vertical bar, turn.

Row 4: With maroon, pull through first lp on hook, (yo, pull through 2 lps on hook) across, **do not turn.**

Row 5: Ch 2, skip first vertical bar, dc lp in top strand of next 4 horizontal bars; for **thumb opening,** ch 4, skip next 4 horizontal bars; dc lp in top strand of each horizontal bar across, turn. *(18 lps on hook) [20 lps on hook, 22 lps on hook]*

Row 6: With green, pull through first lp on hook, ch 3, (pull through 3 lps on hook, ch 2) across to last 2 lps on hook, yo, pull through last 2 lps on hook, **do not turn.**

Row 7: Skip first vertical bar, pull up lp in top strand of each ch across to last vertical bar, pull up lp in last vertical bar, turn. *(21 lps on hook) [23 lps on hook, 25 lps on hook]*

Row 8: With maroon, pull through first lp on hook, (yo, pull through 2 lps on hook) across, **do not turn.**

Row 9: Ch 2, skip next horizontal bar, dc lp in top strand of each horizontal bar across, turn. *(20) [22, 24]*

Row 10: With green, pull through first lp on hook, ch 1, yo, pull through 3 lps on hook, (ch 2, yo, pull through 3 lps on hook) across to last 2 lps on hook, ch 1, yo, pull through last 2 lps on hook, **do not turn.**

Rows 11-19 [11-19, 11-23]: Repeat rows 7-10 consecutively, ending with row 7. At end of last row, **do not turn,** with green, yo, pull through all lps on hook to close, fasten off. Sew ends of rows together.

Thumb

Rnd 1: Working in chs, in ends of rows and in skipped horizontal bars around thumb opening, with K hook, join maroon with sc in any ch, evenly space 9 more sc around, join with sl st in first sc. *(10 sc made)*

Rnds 2-5 [2-6, 2-7]: Ch 1, sc in each st around, join.

Rnd 6 [7, 8]: Ch 1, sc first 2 sts tog, (sc next 2 sts tog) around, join. *(5)* Fasten off. Sew opening closed.

Cuff

Rnd 1: Working in starting ch on opposite side of row 1 on Mitten, with K hook, join maroon with sc in first ch at seam, sc in next 1 [3, 1] st(s), (skip next st, sc in next 3 sts) around, join with sl st in first sc.

Rnds 2-5 [2-6, 2-7]: Ch 1, sc in each st around, join. At end of last rnd, fasten off.

Rnd 6 [7, 8]: With K hook, join green with sl st in first st, ch 1, (sl st in next st, ch 1) around, join with sl st in first sl st. Fasten off.♦

Plant Cozy/Candy Dish

DESIGNED BY SUE PENROD

It only takes a small amount of worsted yarn in festive Christmas colors to create this versatile holiday container that's perfect for a seasonal floral arrangement or colorful candy treats!

FINISHED SIZE: 4" tall.

MATERIALS: 1½ oz. each white and red worsted yarn; 1¾ cup/14 oz. plastic storage container; tapestry needle; H double-ended hook or hook size needed to obtain gauge.

GAUGE: 4 sts = 1"; 7 rows = 1".

NOTES: Read General Instructions on page 6 before beginning pattern.

You may also use any plastic container measuring approximately 4" across bottom x 5½" across top x 2" tall.

CANDY DISH/ PLANT COZY

Row 1: With white, ch 20, pull up lp in second ch from hook, pull up lp in each ch across, turn. *(20 lps on hook)*

Row 2: With red, work lps off hook, **do not turn.**

Row 3: Skip first vertical bar, pull up lp in next 13 vertical bars, pull up lp under last 6 **horizontal bars** *(see illustration)*, turn.

Horizontal Bar

Row 4: With white, work lps off hook, **do not turn.**

Row 5: Skip first vertical bar, pull up lp under next 6 horizontal bars, pull up lp in last 14 vertical bars, turn.

Rows 6-116: Repeat rows 2-5 consecutively, ending with row 4.

Row 117: Skip first vertical bar, sl st in next 13 vertical bars, sl st in last 6 horizontal bars, **do not turn.**

Row 118: Working in ends of rows, ch 1, pull up lp in every other row across, yo, pull through all lps to gather bottom of bowl tightly. Leaving long end for sewing, fasten off. Sew first and last rows together.

Place plastic container inside bottom of crocheted bowl.♦

Pet Bed

DESIGNED BY SUSIE SPIER MAXFIELD

Tuck this plush, cozy bed near the Christmas tree, and the family pet will sleep in snugly comfort as he dreams of all the goodies Santa will bring just for him!

FINISHED SIZE: Cushion is 13" x 18½".

MATERIALS: Worsted yarn—10 oz. green, 8 oz burgundy and 6 oz. white; 4 pieces 7-count plastic canvas each 39 x 90 holes; polyester fiberfill; tapestry needle; J double-ended and H crochet hooks or hook sizes needed to obtain gauges.

GAUGES: With **double-ended hook,** 7 sts worked in Cushion pattern = 2"; 10 rows = 2"; 8 rows worked in Sides pattern = 2½". With **H hook,** 7 sc = 2"; 7 sc rows = 2".

SPECIAL STITCHES: For **dc lp,** yo, pull up lp in next vertical bar, yo, pull through 2 lps on hook.

For **cross stitch (cr st),** skip next vertical bar, dc lp in next vertical bar; working in front of st just made, dc lp in skipped vertical bar.

NOTE: Read General Instructions on page 6 before beginning pattern.

CUSHION
Bottom
Row 1: With H hook and burgundy, ch 36, sc in second ch from hook, sc in each ch across, turn. *(35 sc made)*

Rows 2-6: Ch 1, 2 sc in first st, sc in each st across with 2 sc in last st, turn, ending with *45 sc* in last row.

Rows 7-58: Ch 1, sc in each st across, turn.

Rows 59-63: Ch 1, sc first 2 sts tog, sc in each st across to last 2 sts, sc last 2 sts tog, turn, ending with *35 sc* in last row. At end of last row, **do not turn.**

Rnd 64: For **edging,** working around outer edge, ch 1, sc in each st and in end of each row around, join with sl st in first sc. Fasten off.

Top
Rows 1-7: With H hook and burgundy, repeat same rows of Bottom. At end of last row, change to double-ended hook.

Row 8: Ch 1, skip first st, pull up lp in each st across leaving all lps on hook, turn. *(45 lps on hook)*

Row 9: With green, work lps off hook, **do not turn.**

Row 10: Ch 1, skip first vertical bar, pull up lp in top strand of each **horizontal bar** across *(see illustration)*, turn.

Horizontal Bar

Row 11: With burgundy, work lps off hook, **do not turn.**

Row 12: Ch 1, skip first vertical bar, pull up lp in top strand of each horizontal bar across, turn.

Rows 13-83: Repeat rows 9-12 consecutively, ending with row 11. At end of last row, change to H hook.

Row 84: Ch 1, skip first vertical bar, sc in top strand of each horizontal bar across, turn.

Rows 85-89: Repeat rows 59-63 of Bottom.

Rnd 90: For **edging,** working in sts and in ends of rows around outer edge, evenly spacing sts so piece lays flat, ch 1, sc around, join with sl st in first sc. Fasten off.

Holding Top and Bottom wrong sides together, matching sts and working through both thicknesses, with H hook and burgundy, join with sc in any st, sc in each st around stuffing before closing, join with sl st in first sc. Fasten off.

With tapestry needle and burgundy, insert needle from bottom to top through center of Cushion, make small stitch and pull needle back through to

continued on page 169

Holly Wreath

DESIGNED BY SUE PENROD

Adorn your door with holiday hospitality with this beautiful wreath that's easily created with worsted yarn and a few simple craft materials. Your guests will feel welcomed in the spirit of the season!

FINISHED SIZE: 12" across.

MATERIALS: 3 oz. green worsted yarn; 1 yd. craft ribbon; bow made from desired ribbon; 12" wire wreath form; 5 holly leaf and berry clusters; 5 small pine cones; craft glue or hot glue gun; tapestry needle; H double-ended crochet hook or hook size needed to obtain gauge.

GAUGE: 4 sts = 1"; 7 rows = 1".

NOTES: Read General Instructions on page 6 before beginning pattern.

If using one large skein of green, wind into two separate balls.

WREATH

Row 1: Ch 10, pull up lp in second ch from hook, pull up lp in each ch across, turn. *(10 lps on hook)*

Row 2: With second skein or ball of green, work lps off hook, **do not turn.**

Row 3: Skip first vertical bar, pull up lp under each **horizontal bar** across *(see illustration)*, turn.

Row 4: Work lps off hook, **do not turn.**

Rows 5-200: Repeat rows 3 and 4 alternately.

Row 201: Skip first vertical bar, sl st under each horizontal bar across. Leaving long end for sewing, fasten off. Sew first and last rows together.

Sew over wire wreath form. Decorate as desired using ribbon, bow, holly leaves and pine cones.♦

Pet Bed

continued from page 167

bottom side at beginning, pull to indent, secure with a knot. Make two more indentations on each side of center indentation about 5" from each end of Pillow, ending with a total of five.

SIDES

Row 1: With double-ended hook and green, ch 40, pull up lp in second ch from hook, pull up lp in each ch across, turn. *(40 lps on hook)*

Row 2: With white, work lps off hook, **do not turn.**

Row 3: Ch 1, skip first vertical bar, **cr st** *(see Special Stitches)* across to last vertical bar, **dc lp** *(see Special Stitches)* in last vertical bar, turn.

Row 4: With green, work lps off hook, **do not turn.**

Row 5: Ch 1, skip first vertical bar, cr st across to last vertical bar, dc lp in last vertical bar, turn.

Rows 6-152: Repeat rows 2-5 consecutively, ending with row 4.

Row 153: Ch 1, sc in each vertical bar across. Fasten off.

Rnd 154: For **edging,** working in sts and in end of rows around outer edge, with H hook and white, join with sc in first st, evenly spacing sts so piece lays flat, sc around, join with sl st in first sc. Fasten off.

With tapestry needle and white, sew short ends of plastic canvas together forming one long piece. Place on top of crocheted sides; trim to same length as crochet piece.

Fold crocheted Sides over plastic canvas piece, working through both thicknesses, with H hook, join white with sc in first st after fold on one end, sc in each st around to fold on opposite end enclosing plastic canvas completely. Fasten off.

Sew sts on bottom edging of Sides around outer edge of Cushion centering an opening in front of Cushion as shown in photo. Tack top edge of Cushion Top to inside edge of Sides.♦

Candy Canes Baby Afghan

DESIGNED BY MARY ANN SIPES

Candy canes dance in sweet baby dreams when you wrap your little one in this yummy afghan confection crocheted in a charming, reversible pattern with baby-soft sport weight yarn.

FINISHED SIZE: 30½" x 50".

MATERIALS: 3-ply sport yarn—12 oz. white and 11 oz. red; G double-ended and F crochet hook or hook sizes needed to obtain gauge.

GAUGE: 5 sts = 1"; 6 rows = 1".

SPECIAL STITCH: For **cluster (cl),** yo, pull up lp in specified vertical bar 4 rows below, yo, pull through 2 lps on hook, (yo, pull up lp in same bar, yo, pull through 2 lps on hook) 2 times, yo, pull through 3 lps on hook. Skip next horizontal bar on last row.

NOTE: Read General Instructions on page 6 before beginning pattern.

AFGHAN

Row 1: With white, ch 124, pull up lp in second ch from hook, pull up lp in each ch across, turn. *(124 lps on hook)*

Row 2: With red, work lps off hook, **do not turn.**

Row 3: Skip first vertical bar, pull up lp in top strand of each **horizontal bar** across *(see illustration),* turn.

Horizontal Bar

Row 4: With white, work lps off hook, **do not turn.**

Row 5: Skip first vertical bar, pull up lp in top strand of each horizontal bar across, turn.

Rows 6-8: Repeat rows 2-4.

Row 9: Skip first vertical bar, pull up lp in top strand of next 9 horizontal bars, **cl** *(see Special Stitch)* in twelfth vertical bar 4 rows below, (pull up lp in top strand of next 12 horizontal bars on last row, skip next 12 vertical bars 4 rows below, cl in next vertical bar) 8 times, pull up lp in top strand of last 9 horizontal bars, turn.

Row 10: With red, work lps off hook, **do not turn.**

Row 11: Repeat row 9.

Row 12: With white, work lps off hook, **do not turn.**

Row 13: Skip first vertical bar, pull up lp in top strand of next 8 horizontal bars, cl in tenth vertical bar 4 rows below, (pull up lp in top strand of next 12 horizontal bars on last row, skip next 12 vertical bars 4 rows below, cl in next vertical bar) 8 times, pull up lp in top strand of last 10 horizontal bars, turn.

Row 14: With red, work lps off hook, **do not turn.**

Row 15: Repeat row 13.

Row 16: With white, work lps off hook, **do not turn.**

Row 17: Skip first vertical bar, pull up lp in top strand of next 7 horizontal bars, cl in ninth vertical bar 4 rows below, (pull up lp in top strand of next 12 horizontal bars on last row, skip next 12 vertical bars 4 rows below, cl in next vertical bar) 8 times, pull up lp in top strand of last 11 horizontal bars, turn.

Row 18: With red, work lps off hook, **do not turn.**

Row 19: Repeat row 17.

Row 20: With white, work lps off hook, **do not turn.**

Row 21: Skip first vertical bar, pull up lp in top strand of next 6 horizontal bars, (*cl in eighth vertical bar 4 rows below, pull up lp in top strand of next 3 horizontal bars on last row, skip next 2 vertical bars 4 rows below, cl in next vertical bar*, pull up lp in top strand of next 8 horizontal bars on last row, skip next 8 vertical bars 4 rows below) 8 times; repeat between **, pull up lp in

continued on page 175

Evening Top

DESIGNED BY ANN PARNELL

A combination of baby yarn and metallic thread creates the sparkling elegance in this classic-style top. Whether paired with evening pants or a skirt, it's sure to add just the right touch of glitz and glamour to your holiday wardrobe!

FINISHED SIZES: Instructions given fit women's 34" bust (small). Changes for 38" (medium), 42" (large) and 46" (X-large) busts are in [ ].

MATERIALS: 5 [5½, 6, 6½] oz. each white fingering baby yarn; 700 [800, 900, 1000] yds. black/silver crochet cotton thread; tapestry needle; F crochet and G double-ended hooks or hook size needed to obtain gauge.

GAUGE: With **double-ended hook,** 3 shells = 1"; 10 rows = 1".

NOTES: Read General Instructions on page 6 before beginning pattern.

Use double-ended hook unless otherwise stated.

Work all even numbered rows loosely .

Tie a knot in ends of crochet thread rows when beginning or ending, so the silver will not ravel.

TOP
Back

Row 1: Starting at bottom, with white, ch 105 [117, 129, 141], pull up lp in second ch from hook, pull up lp in each ch across, turn. *(105 lps on hook)* [*117 lps on hook, 129 lps on hook, 141 lps on hook*]

Row 2: With black, yo, pull through one lp on hook, *ch 1, yo, pull through 3 lps on hook *(completes a ch 2 and a shell);* repeat from * across, **do not turn.**

Row 3: Ch 1, pull up lp in each ch across, turn. *(105 lps on hook)* [*117 lps on hook, 129 lps on hook, 141 lps on hook*]

Row 4: With white, yo, pull through one lp on hook, *ch 1, yo, pull through 3 lps on hook *(completes a ch 2 and a shell);* repeat from * across, **do not turn.**

Row 5: Ch 1, pull up lp in each ch across, turn.

Rows 6-108 [6-112, 6-116, 6-120]: Repeat rows 2-5 consecutively, ending with row 4.

Row 109 [113, 117, 121]: For **sleeve shaping,** ch 3, pull up lp in second ch from hook, pull up lp in next ch; working on last row, pull up lp in

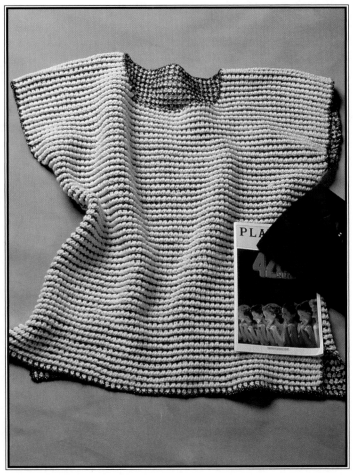

each ch across, turn. *(107 lps on hook) [119 lps on hook, 131 lps on hook, 143 lps on hook]*

Row 110 [114, 118, 122]: With black, yo, pull through one lp on hook, *ch 1, yo, pull through 3 lps on hook *(completes a ch 2 and a shell)*; repeat from * across, **do not turn.**

Row 111 [115, 119, 123]: Ch 3, pull up lp in second ch from hook, pull up lp in next ch; working on last row, pull up lp in each ch across, turn. *(109 lps on hook) [121 lps on hook, 133 lps on hook, 145 lps on hook]*

Row 112 [116, 120, 124]: With white, yo, pull through one lp on hook, *ch 1, yo, pull through 3 lps on hook *(completes a ch 2 and a shell)*; repeat from * across, **do not turn.**

Row 113 [117, 121, 125]: Ch 1, pull up lp in each ch across, turn.

Row 114 [118, 122, 126]: With black, yo, pull through one lp on hook, *ch 1, yo, pull through 3 lps on hook *(completes a ch 2 and a shell)*; repeat from * across, **do not turn.**

Row 115 [119, 123, 127]: Ch 1, pull up lp in each ch across, turn.

Row 116 [120, 124, 128]: With white, yo, pull through one lp on hook, *ch 1, yo, pull through 3 lps on hook *(completes a ch 2 and a shell)*; repeat from * across, **do not turn.**

Rows 117-164 [121-168, 125-172, 129-176]: Repeat rows 109-116 [113-120, 117-124, 121-128] consecutively. At end of last row *(133 lps on hook) [145 lps on hook, 157 lps on hook, 169 lps on hook].*

Row 165 [169, 173, 177]: Repeat row 5.

Rows 166-226 [170-234, 174-242, 178-250]: Repeat rows 2-5 consecutively ending with row 2. At end of last row, fasten off.

Front

Rows 1-165 [1-169, 1-173, 1-177]: Repeat rows 1-165 [1-169, 1-173, 1-177] of Back.

Rows 166-184 [170-192, 174-200, 178-208]: Repeat rows 2-5 of Back consecutively, ending with row 4.

Row 185 [193, 201, 209]: For **first shoulder,** ch 1, pull up lp in next 48 [54, 60, 66] chs leaving remaining chs unworked, turn. *(49 lps on hook) [55 lps on hook, 61 lps on hook, 67 lps on hook]*

Row 186 [194, 202, 210]: With black, yo, pull

through one lp on hook, *ch 1, yo, pull through 3 lps on hook *(completes a ch-2 and a shell)*; repeat from * across, **do not turn.**

Row 187 [195, 203, 211]: Ch 1, (pull up lp in next ch, skip next ch) 2 times, pull up lp in each remaining ch across, turn. *(47 lps on hook) [53 lps on hook, 59 lps on hook, 65 lps on hook]*

Row 188 [196, 204, 212]: With white, yo, pull through one lp on hook, *ch 1, yo, pull through 3 lps on hook *(completes a ch-2 and a shell)*; repeat from * across, **do not turn.**

Row 189 [197, 205, 213]: Ch 1, pull up lp in each ch across, turn.

Row 190-197 [198-205, 206-213, 214-221]: Repeat rows 186-189 [194-197, 202-205, 210-213] consecutively. At end of last row, *(43 lps on hook) [49 lps on hook, 55 lps on hook, 61 lps on hook].*

Row 198-226 [206-234, 214-242, 222-250]: Repeat rows 2-5 of Back consecutively ending with row 2. At end of last row, fasten off.

Row 185 [193, 201, 209]: For **second shoulder,** with predominately black side facing you, skip next 34 chs on row 184 [192, 200, 208], with white, pull up lp in next ch, skip next ch, pull up lp in each remaining ch across, turn. *(49 lps on hook) [55 lps on hook, 61 lps on hook, 67 lps on hook]*

Rows 186 [194, 202, 210]: With black, yo, pull through one lp on hook, *ch 1, yo, pull through 3 lps on hook *(completes a ch-2 and a shell)*; repeat from * across, **do not turn.**

Row 187 [195, 203, 211]: Ch 1, pull up lp in each ch across to last 4 chs, (skip next ch, pull up lp in next ch) 2 times *(decrease made)*, turn. *(47 lps on hook) [53 lps on hook, 59 lps on hook, 65 lps on hook]*

Row 188 [196, 204, 212]: With white, yo, pull through one lp on hook, *ch 1, yo, pull through 3 lps on hook *(completes a ch-2 and a shell)*; repeat from * across, **do not turn.**

Row 189 [197, 205, 213]: Ch 1, pull up lp in each ch across, turn.

Rows 190-197 [198-205, 206-213, 214-221]: Repeat rows 186-189 [194-197, 202-205, 210-213] of second shoulder consecutively. At end of last row *(43 lps on hook) [49 lps on hook, 55 lps on hook, 61 lps on hook]*

Row 198-226 [206-234, 214-242, 222-250]: Repeat rows 2-5 consecutively, ending with row 2. At end of last row, fasten off.

With predominantly white side facing you, match and sew sts on Front and Back shoulders together with black.

Starting 3" from bottom edge on Front and Back sides, sew side seams up to sleeve shaping.

Neck Trim

With predominantly black side facing, with F hook and black, join with sc in any seam on neckline, evenly spacing sts so piece lays flat, sc around, join with sl st in first sc. Fasten off.

Sleeve Trim

With predominantly black side facing, with F hook and black, join with sc in seam at underarm of one Sleeve, evenly spacing sts so piece lays flat, sc around, join with sl st in first sc. Fasten off.

Bottom Trim

With predominantly black side facing, with F hook and black, working in ends of rows and in starting ch on opposite side of row 1, join with sc in any seam, evenly spacing sts so piece lays flat, sc around with 4 sc in each corner, join with sl st in first sc. Fasten off.♦

Candy Canes Baby Afghan

continued from page 171

top strand of last 8 horizontal bars, turn.

Row 22: With red, work lps off hook, **do not turn.**

Row 23: Repeat row 21.

Row 24: With white, work lps off hook, **do not turn.**

Row 25: Skip first vertical bar, pull up lp in top strand of next 7 horizontal bars, (*cl in first vertical bar after next cl 4 rows below, pull up lp in top strand of next horizontal bar on last row, skip next vertical bar 4 rows below, cl in next vertical bar*, pull up lp in top strand of next 10 horizontal bars on last row) 8 times; repeat between **, pull up lp in top strand of last 9 horizontal bars on last row, turn.

Row 26: With red, work lps off hook, **do not turn.**

Row 27: Repeat row 25.

Row 28: With white, work lps off hook, **do not turn.**

Row 29: Repeat row 5.

Rows 30-36: Repeat rows 2-5 consecutively, ending with row 4.

Rows 37-308: Repeat rows 9-36 consecutively, ending with row 28.

Row 309: Ch 1, sl st in each vertical bar across. Fasten off red; **do not fasten off** white.

BORDER

*NOTES: For **beginning cluster (beg cl)**, ch 3, (yo, insert hook in same st or sp, yo, pull lp through, yo, pull through 2 lps on hook) 2 times, yo, pull through all 3 lps on hook.*

*For **cluster (cl) for remainder of pattern**, yo, insert hook in next st or ch sp, yo, pull lp through, yo, pull through 2 lps on hook, (yo, insert hook in same st or sp, yo, pull lp through, yo, pull through 2 lps on hook) 2 times, yo, pull through all 4 lps on hook.*

Rnd 1: Working in rnds, with F hook and white, with white candy canes on Afghan facing you, (beg cl, ch 3, cl) in last st on this row; working in ends of rows, ch 1, skip next red stripe, (cl in next white stripe, ch 1, skip next red stripe across; working in starting ch on opposite side of row 1, (cl, ch 3, cl) in first ch, skip next 2 chs, (cl in next ch, ch 1, skip next 2 chs) across to last ch, (cl, ch 3, cl) in last ch; working in ends of rows, ch 1, skip next red stripe, (cl in next white stripe, ch 1, skip next red stripe) across; working in sts across last row, (cl, ch 3, cl) in first st, skip next 2 sts, (cl in next st, ch 1, skip next 2 sts) across, join with sl st in top of beg cl, **turn.** Fasten off.

Rnd 2: Join red with sl st in any corner ch sp, (beg cl, ch 3, cl) in same sp, ch 1, (cl in next ch sp, ch 1) around with (cl, ch 3, cl) in each corner ch sp, join, **turn.** Fasten off.

Rnd 3: With white, repeat rnd 2.♦

The Crochet On the Double™ hooks and Crochenit™ hooks can be purchased from local craft, fabric and variety stores or from the Annie's Attic Needlecraft Catalog by calling 1-800-582-6643 or by visiting AnniesAttic.com.

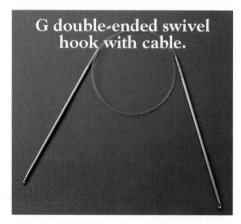

Crochet On the Double hooks and Crochet On the Double swivel hooks are available in sizes G, H and K.

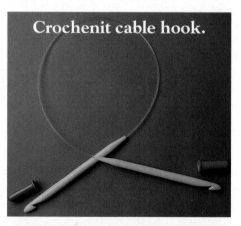

Crochenit cable hook.

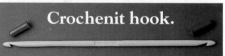

Crochenit hook.